WHAT PEOPLE ABOUT *THE HONOR KEY*

"Russell Evans' book on honor is such an important tool in the hands of the church today. Leaders who want a culture of honor so they'll be treated better miss the point. Honor is the atmosphere in which the people of God become their best. Russell has done a great job in highlighting the importance of honor as a vital key to creating a kingdom culture. Receiving and giving honor enables us to walk as true sons and daughters of God, restored to our rightful place, to see heaven released in and through our lives."

—*Bill Johnson*
Senior Leader of Bethel Church, Redding, California
Author of *When Heaven Invades Earth* and *Hosting the Presence*

"I'm so grateful God used Russell Evans to bring us this vital message about a neglected key to understanding the heart of God and the way His kingdom functions. Pastor Evans' gift for making vital concepts clear, accessible, and actionable shines through on every page of *The Honor Key*. I recommend this book wholeheartedly."

—*Robert Morris*
Founding Senior Pastor, Gateway Church, Dallas, Texas
Best-selling author of *The Blessed Life, From Dream to Destiny,* and *The God I Never Knew*

"Pastor Russell Evans is one of the preeminent voices in global youth culture and revival. His insights into leadership and church development are not the cold pontifications of an ivy-tower-bound postulator but have been ground tested and proven in the real-world laboratory of leading both a church and a youth movement that are impacting the world.

"In His new book, *The Honor Key*, Russell Evans shares with us a vital key to the advancement of the kingdom in modern culture—honor. He dares to challenge the current tepid temperature of religious relationships and calls us to foster genuine connectivity through the Spirit of Honor. This book is required reading for anyone desiring to understand relevant, relational currency in the rising church."

—DR. CHRIS HILL
Senior Pastor, The Potter's House of Denver, Colorado

"History always proves a principle to be right or wrong. In a relatively short time, Pastor Russell Evans has proven that history is on his side, validating the kingdom principle of *honor*, which he practices as a lifestyle. His book *The Honor Key* will change your life. Through his unique conversational style, you will discover foundational keys to unlocking heaven over your life and walking in personal destiny. Every person who reads this book will be inspired to discover, pursue, and fulfill their unique God-given calling."

—JENTEZEN FRANKLIN
Senior Pastor, Free Chapel, Gainesville, Georgia
Author of *New York Times* best-seller, *Fasting*

"There are few men I know who are as qualified as Russell Evans to write on the subject of honor. What you will read in these pages is not just theory but is modeled and lived out daily in the life of Russell and in the community called Planetshakers. I have personally been greatly impacted by the culture of honor at Planetshakers. They are a testimony of what God intends to do in cities across the earth. The issue of honor is one the church must get right if we are to fulfill our mandate to see nations transformed. Few subjects can bring such radical change in an environment as properly understanding honor. I am grateful Russell has tackled this subject. The church will be strengthened because of it, and nations will be transformed."

—*BANNING LIEBSCHER*
SLT/Director, Jesus Culture

"I love Russell Evans' new book, *The Honor Key*. His engaging life stories and clear teaching reveal how honor is the foundation of the kingdom that unlocks the possibilities of heaven. It will literally change the atmosphere of your life. I now look at every person and situation differently . . . from honor's view . . . God's view. I highly recommend this book."

—*JOHN MASON*
Author of *An Enemy Called Average* and many other best-selling books

"Pastor Russell Evans doesn't sugar coat anything! This is as real as it gets. *The Honor Key* is one of those rare books that illuminates key biblical and kingdom principles in a way we can all apply to our everyday lives. Planetshakers Awakening (conference) grew from 300 to around 25,000 people in a few short years based on the biblical wisdom and truth contained in these pages. Pastor Russell shares openly about the intimate experiences of both triumph and struggle in his private and public ministry life. *The Honor Key* will encourage you to stay strong and committed, and move forward on the journey God has called you. I dare you to read it! It's more than what you think."

—MILES MCPHERSON
Founder and Senior Pastor of Rock Church, San Diego, California
Author of *God in the Mirror*

"I've known Russell for many years, and he truly is a man of honor, which makes this book even more powerful because it's written from the platform of his life and convictions. I believe you'll see that honor is the key to establishing strong, harmonious relationships with our families, our friends, co-workers, and our churches. To use Russell's own words, "Honor is the opposite of control, because control is all about me, and honor is all about us." You're going to love this book!"

—MARK CROW
Senior Pastor, Victory Church, Oklahoma City, Oklahoma
Author of *Extraordinary Living, Mastering Your Storms,* and *The Secrets of the Second Mile*

"*The Honor Key* is full of truth! Pastor Russell Evans has delivered a powerful message in a day and age when our culture is lacking in honor. What a fresh way to remind us of the importance of honor and what it can unlock in our lives!"

—CINDY CRUSE RATCLIFF
Senior Worship Leader, Lakewood Church, Houston, Texas, Joel Osteen Ministries

"If you're looking to go deeper and wider in your faith, Pastor Russell's book will equip you with the spiritual tools to become the honorable person God has created you to be. His book is beyond insightful—he shares his heart and wisdom on how to honor God in your everyday walk and through life's difficult choices and circumstances."

—WILFREDO DE JESUS
Senior Pastor New Life Covenant Church Chicago, Illinois
Author of *Amazing Faith* and included in 2013 *Time 100: The Most Influential People in the World*

"The principles of living a life of honoring God above all else are clearly laid out in Pastor Russell Evans' new book. With *The Honor Key*, Evans has lifted the veil over this important subject and given his readers new insight into an authentic and blessed life. After all is said and done, we know this from his wonderful book: 'As the heavens and all therein raise their voices in honor and praise to God, we are to do likewise' (Revelation 4:11)."

—MARCUS D. LAMB
Founder and President, Daystar Television Network

"Pastor Russell Evans is undoubtedly one of the great leaders God is raising up in our generation! His ministry through Planetshakers is reshaping the face of music in the church around the globe, and his dynamic prophetic voice is an inspiration to the body of Christ to return to God's order of living spirit-filled and victorious! Pastor Russell is a focused, passionate man of God, and I know this book is filled with wisdom and insight that will challenge you to live for God's glory and to become everything He intends for you to be!"

—PASTOR AT BOSHOFF
Senior Pastor, Christian Revival Church, Blomfontein,
Free State Province, South Africa
Author of *Dream Stealers* and *Live a Yes Life*

"People around the world are blessed by the fruit of Russell Evans' Planetshakers ministry—it impacts the world in a unique and powerful way. I've ministered with Planetshakers in Australia, USA, Philippines, and Malaysia. The impact is always life-changing. *The Honor Key* eloquently unpacks the foundational key that enables a life where Jesus truly is the center of it all. If you want to unlock a limitless life in Christ, this book is for you."

—ISRAEL HOUGHTON
Internationally recognized worship leader, recording artist, producer, and Grammy Award-winning musician and songwriter; gold-selling albums include "The Power of One" and "A Deeper Level"

THE HONOR KEY
Unlock a Limitless Life

Russell Evans

MY HEALTHY CHURCH
MyHealthyChurch.com

MY HEALTHY CHURCH
MyHealthyChurch.com

Published by My Healthy Church
1445 North Boonville Avenue
Springfield, Missouri 65802

Cover design by Sheepish Design (www.sheepishdesign.com)
Cover image of New York City skyline is licensed from Shutterstock.
Used by permission. www.shutterstock.com

Interior design by Prodigy Pixel (www.prodigypixel.com)

ISBN: 978-1-62423-102-5
Printed in the United States of America
17 16 15 14 • 1 2 3 4 5

CONTENTS

FOREWORD

We live in a world that is obsessed with success. Advertisers promise it—if you'll buy their latest products. Leaders and influencers use it to justify compromise and self-serving behavior. And too often we hear stories about those who have sought their own success at the expense of others.

God loves success. "I want," He told His people, "to prosper you" (see Jeremiah 29:11). Adhering to His wisdom guarantees it, for wisdom boasts, "Common sense and success belong to me" (Proverbs 8:14, NLT). But God defines success differently. He defines it not according to the understanding of the world but according to His eternal wisdom. Paul wrote, "God has made the wisdom of this world look foolish" (1 Corinthians 1:20 NLT).

So instead of encouraging us to fight our way to the top or demand opportunities, God speaks to the destiny inside each of us and tells us what we must do to release it: honor. We must honor God, others, and even ourselves according to the identity our Creator has given us. When we choose the path of honor, we position ourselves for blessing and eternal success. Honor is a key to success, yet somehow there is a shortage of good books on this vital subject.

My friend Russell Evans has seen success in his life and ministry. Untold millions have been impacted forever by his faithfulness. I know this man and his heart. I can tell you (and he would agree) that his story is a story of God's grace—a grace that is freely given to those who rely on God.

Though your story is unique to you, if you will be attentive to the timeless principles in this book, you will find deeper conviction to seek the reward of God's presence. As you spend time in His presence, you will be transformed into the extraordinary, favored, and powerful child of God you were created to be.

As Russell shares in this book, God's kingdom celebrates each individual, but it is a family affair. While worldly success is often oriented toward self, your success in God is about so much more than you. God's desire is to see you fulfilled, others invested in, and ultimately, Himself glorified. By His Spirit and His Word, He is more than able to accomplish this in and through you. Your role is to receive from and partner with Him.

The personal stories and biblical truths you will find on these pages will bring you encouragement and position you for revelation. This book will call you into a life of grace, found only through relationship with the One who is its source. Press in. Choose to believe. Have the faith to follow . . . and enjoy the journey!

JOHN BEVERE
Author of *Honor's Reward* and *The Bait of Satan*
Messenger International
Colorado Springs / United Kingdom / Australia

INTRODUCTION

I want to honor you for selecting this book. It's a life message, not just a thought. I've begun the journey of honor and am still on it, so I want to honor you for coming on that journey with me.

If God can take a terribly insecure pastor's kid (which I was) and reveal to him a key to His kingdom, He can do the same for you. There are many things I've gleaned from my spiritual life, and I would love to share some of those with you and help you walk out your own destiny, your own calling.

God has made you in His image—you are unique and valuable to His kingdom. He has created gifts and abilities in your life, but to see those gifts and abilities come to fulfillment, it takes risk. It takes vulnerability, trust, and faith.

It takes honor.

As you open the pages of this book, I dare you to discover the power of the kingdom of God that can come into your life through the principle of honor. When you do, it will release an inheritance. A generational blessing will come out of your life that will affect not only your life but the lives of those around you for years to come.

I honor you for taking the risk to open the cover, read the first page, and then the next page and the next. I honor you for daring to discover the journey of a life of honor.

CHAPTER 1

GOD OF HONOR

I f you're like me, you want to experience heaven here on earth. You want to have abundance, receive an inheritance, and release generational blessings. Basically, you desire to lead a more effective Christian life.

So are you experiencing these things? In your life today, are you walking in all the peace, prosperity, and freedom you'll experience in heaven?

If you hesitated for a moment, or know for sure you're not, the first question that must come to mind is, "Why not?"

I asked myself this question, and the answer I received from God was not at all what I expected. There are many principles in the Bible God uses to bless us, but He showed me something beneath the surface explanations I had heard that formed a bedrock for everything else.

Under faith, hope, and love, and beneath walking in obedience and making room for the Holy Spirit in our lives, and undergirding kingdom principles is a key. It's a foundational truth throughout God's Word that's found in every action of the Father, Son, and Holy Spirit.

That truth is honor.

All through the Bible, the value of honor is the essence of the kingdom of God. In fact, I believe that honor is the foundational truth of the kingdom. Everything revolves around this topic of honor. Everything happens because of honor. As I examined the life of Jesus, I saw something quite interesting. Every miracle, every breakthrough, indeed everything that happened in His life actually happened when people honored what He carried or honored the miracles He performed or honored who He was.

Honor affects every part of your life. A lifestyle of honor affects your marriage, your family, your job, your finances, and your church life. In fact, it affects everything.

Many Christians are familiar with the term *honor,* and some can even quote Scriptures on the subject, such as, "Honor your father and your mother, so that you may live long in the land the LORD your God is giving you" (Exodus 20:12). Unfortunately, many people have a misconception of honor. Or they have a narrow view of honor. We often misuse the term because we don't understand what honor really means.

We readily think of honor in terms of Scripture verses that tell us to honor our father and mother, and in some circles pastors and leaders have used the terms *honor* and *submit* interchangeably when talking about how to respond to authority. Because of partial understandings and misunderstandings about honor, many people become frustrated and drop the term entirely from their lives.

However, God showed me a different perspective on honor, and in this book I hope to help you begin the journey of a life of honor. I don't claim to have it all figured out or to have mastered this concept, but what the Lord has shown me is important to any Christian who desires to live a kingdom-centered life.

Just a moment ago, I asked you to consider why you aren't experiencing heaven on earth as you would like. The answer God gave me for my own life when I asked this same question was striking: "Because there's no honor."

But then He showed me something else: In everyday life, a lifestyle of honor brings heaven to earth.

The Honoring Father

The word *honor* actually means "to esteem at the highest level" or "to add weight to." It comes from the time when people used to weigh shekels (coins) to determine their value. The heavier the coin, the more value it had. And so it is with honor—the more you put value on something, the more weight it has in your life.

When we honor someone or something, we give it weight or deep respect. It isn't enough to feel it inside; honor must include an outward expression or it's just lip service (Isaiah 29:13). Honor includes the heart condition and the outward expression of respect and reverence for something that we esteem to the highest degree.

HONOR INCLUDES THE HEART CONDITION AND THE OUTWARD EXPRESSION OF RESPECT AND REVERENCE FOR SOMETHING THAT WE ESTEEM TO THE HIGHEST DEGREE.

In order to understand biblical honor, we need to look at God for a perfect demonstration of this powerful kingdom principle. As sovereign Creator, He is the original source of honor. I had never thought of honor in the way the Lord has been showing me. To explain it as He showed me, I want to use a story you probably know, but I believe you will see in a different way when we're done.

One of the stories I love most in the Bible is the story of the prodigal son (which I think is misnamed, as I will explain later). You may know it well, but allow me to frame this story in a new light.

The younger son demanded his inheritance from his father and left for a distant land. To begin with, asking his father for his inheritance was an act of dishonor. He then proceeded to live wildly and spend his inheritance. He lived a life centered on doing whatever he wanted to do and on spending his money frivolously—until it ran out.

The money was gone, and so was all the food. It was a time of famine, and he didn't have enough to eat. With no money, no friends, and nothing to eat, he hit rock bottom. When he envied some pigs eating their dinner, he realized that even the servants in his father's house at least had enough to eat. So he came to his senses and started for home.

Imagine for a moment that you were in the shoes of the prodigal son as he arrived at the outer gate of his father's property, starving and dirty. The last time he passed through that gate, he was sure he could make it alone in the world. He couldn't wait to break free from his dad's rules. Life was awesome for a while, probably even better than he had imagined. He was surrounded by people who thought he was cool (as long as he had money), but eventually starvation, humiliation, and regret were his only friends.

I imagine he rehearsed over and over in his mind what he would say to his dad to convince him to let him come back home—not as a son, but as a servant. He probably dreaded the reactions of the rest of the family and even the servants who had once served him. But though humiliating, these things probably seemed worth it for the relief of coming back under his father's covering and provision.

We learn that the father had been waiting every day for his son to return home. When he saw his son, he could have said, "Hey son, you really messed up your life. You've caused me great pain." But instead, the father saw the young man while he was still a long way off and *ran* to him. He greeted and embraced his son.

Then the father did something that seems strange to us— the father *honored* the son. The heart of the father was moved to *honor* his rebellious son. He reacted the opposite way that everyone expected him to. He didn't shout at his son or remind him of the great dishonor and humiliation his behavior had brought on his father and his household. He didn't mention the financial cost or the shameful activities the son had participated in while living the high life.

No, the father showed nothing but genuine love and honor toward his son.

Jesus used this parable to cut through the lies and misunderstandings about the nature of His Father. This confronting story undermines the teachings of religious people who try to keep others in bondage and fear by teaching that God is an angry God who responds to sin with judgment and punishment.

Jesus used the story to declare that the opposite is true: Regardless of our condition, God always waits with love, forgiveness, and honor for all who are willing to humble themselves and reach out to Him.

A Robe, a Ring, and Some Sandals

God is by nature "honor" just as He is by nature "love," and we see these character traits expressed consistently in everything He says and does. In this story Jesus shows the heart of our heavenly Father toward each of us.

After tasting the bitter dregs of life in the world and discovering his father's wisdom to be true, the son found himself at a turning point in life. He realized his own foolishness and approached his dad differently—with honor (weighty respect and courtesy). This was the change of heart the father had been waiting so long to see, and he was overcome with joy. In response to his son's humility, the father engaged in three actions that clearly communicated his feelings for his lost son—now found—that are highly symbolic for us.

First, he placed a robe on him. This act represents restored honor and dignity. No longer was the evidence of the son's sin in full view for all to see. No longer was his shame and filth exposed and displayed. Kings, priests, and people of influence wore this kind of robe. By placing one on his son, the father communicated to everyone that his son was restored to the position he once held.

This is a beautiful picture of the "robe of righteousness" that is placed on all who receive Jesus as their Lord and Savior (Isaiah 61:10). This is God's way of communicating to us that He no longer sees our past and our failures but only the authority and favor He originally placed on us.

> REGARDLESS OF OUR CONDITION, GOD ALWAYS WAITS WITH LOVE, FORGIVENESS, AND HONOR FOR ALL WHO ARE WILLING TO HUMBLE THEMSELVES AND REACH OUT TO HIM.

Second, the father put a ring on his son's finger. This act symbolized the restoration of the son's full authority in the father's household. It was not dependent on the son's *behavior*, but on his rightful *position* as son. When he honored his father, it restored his authority.

Third, the father put sandals on his son's feet. This act symbolized the way the father wanted his son to walk: not as a slave, but as a son. Because slaves didn't wear sandals, they were easily distinguished from those in authority. By covering the young man's feet, the father communicated his restored position as son.

Here's another thing I noticed from this story. After restoring his son, the father said to his servants, "Kill the fattened calf! We're having a celebration!" I think that from the moment the son left, his dad planned for the day he'd come home and had a calf prepared for the celebration. It was a fattened calf. He didn't say, "Get me a calf." He said, "Get the *fattened* calf." He had been waiting for the day he could honor his son—such was the heart of the father.

And such is the heart of our heavenly Father.

Our Honoring Father

Like me, I'm sure you're amazed and moved by this honoring father's love, devotion, and heart of restoration toward his son. Imagine what this welcome did for the relationship between the prodigal son and his father! Imagine the relief and gratitude that flooded that son's heart. Imagine how he loved his father.

Does this sound familiar? This is a picture of the amazing experience of "coming home" to our heavenly Father when we choose to accept Jesus into our lives. Let's wander down memory lane for a moment.

Do you remember hitting rock bottom in your life as guilt, shame, and self-hatred overwhelmed you? Do you remember the moment you decided that anything would be better than the pit you were living in? Do you remember crying out to God in desperation, hoping that He wouldn't ignore you like you deserved?

Do you remember?

Then it happened—He responded like the father in this story. He didn't respond in the way you expected Him to, did He? Do you remember how you felt accepted and loved? Do you remember how you felt valued and important to someone—something you hadn't felt in such a long time? Do you remember how unworthy you felt when He forgave you, favored you, and spoke incredible promises into your heart? Promises that brought hope to your future? Do you remember the joy and gratitude you felt in response to His unbelievable kindness in the face of your failures?

Do you remember?

This is our God. He practices honor, and He attracts honor. He is honor.

Without honor, you cannot come to salvation. God has honored us just as the father in this story honored his wayward son. But in return, we must honor God in order to receive His gift of salvation and restoration. The way through the door of salvation is honor, and the way of living once you're through the door of salvation is also honor.

> *THE WAY THROUGH THE DOOR OF SALVATION IS HONOR, AND THE WAY OF LIVING ONCE YOU'RE THROUGH THE DOOR OF SALVATION IS ALSO HONOR.*

If we truly desire to become more like our heavenly Father, we must model ourselves on His character. What He loves, we must love; and what He honors, we must honor. If your heart is soft and you're willing to allow God to change you from the inside out, then come with me on this journey of discovery. You will be changed forever as we uncover the powerful truth about honor and see God's "kingdom come" in our lives.

They call this story the parable of the prodigal son, but it really should be named the parable of the honoring father. Jesus wanted to present the facts about His Father so people could walk in truth, life, and freedom regardless of their mistakes. That's why He revealed His Father's heart. It was completely different from what the religious establishment thought God was like. Jesus showed that His Father embraces honor, even for wayward sons.

He hasn't changed.

CHAPTER 2

WHERE HONOR STARTS

A frequent misconception about honor is where it starts. Those who misuse the term primarily feel that honor is due to them. They're willing to receive honor but aren't willing to give it, as the father of the prodigal son gave it to his wayward boy. In actuality, honor flows in every direction in our lives, both up to those in authority above us and down to those for whom we have responsibility.

But where does honor *start?*

I'd like to go back to the parable of the prodigal son we talked about in the first chapter. When we look at this story, it's clear to me that honor begins with the father—and even more specifically, Jesus shows us that honor begins with His Father. In Luke 15:20, we read, "But while he was still a long way off, his father saw him and was filled with compassion for him; he ran to his son, threw his arms around him and kissed him." Before the son could say one word, the father disregarded his Jewish dignity and *ran* to him, threw his arms around him, and kissed him—he honored him. *Then* the son responded with honor in turn: "Father, I have sinned against heaven and against you. I am no longer worthy to be called your son" (Luke 15:21).

So our heavenly Father is the One who releases honor to us, first and continually. We simply must choose to respond.

DREAMS AND AMBITIONS ARE GREAT, BUT WHEN WE LINK FAITH TO ACTION THROUGH HONOR, WE UNLOCK THE GIFTS GOD HAS PUT INTO OUR LIVES.

As a father, I release honor into my house, and because I honor my children, I want to bless them. I want to help them develop their lives. My son, Jonathan, wanted to learn to play basketball when he was eight, and since I love sports, I was eager to teach him. The problem was, he preferred to get his lessons from the Xbox. He lived in the world of video games. He thought he was LeBron James or Kobe Bryant, and he tried to be that person on the basketball court. But he didn't want to practice actually playing basketball—he wanted to gain basketball skills by osmosis and "practice" by playing Xbox.

I remember when I took him to play his first basketball game. He came home disappointed—even a little mad. He hadn't scored or gotten any rebounds. I sat him down and explained, "Jonathan, the reason you're not able to do those things is that you've been living your life on a screen. You're not living it on the court."

"What do you mean?" he asked.

"How did LeBron or Kobe get to be such good players?" I asked. I answered for him: "Practice."

Well, the first time I told him that, he totally ignored it and kept playing on the Xbox instead of practicing on the court. The next game he didn't do well again, and he was frustrated once more.

"The only way you're going to develop basketball skill is to get off the couch and onto the court to practice basketball," I told him—while he was playing Xbox.

But this time he did something different—he honored me. "Yes, dad," he replied. He started practicing his shooting. In fact, he worked on it all week.

I watched him practice and encouraged him. The day of his next game I said, "How many points are we believing for today? How many do you think you can get?"

"Ten?" he responded.

"Okay, you've honored what I said and practiced, so now let's go out and do it!" I gave him a high five.

That day when we drove home, he had a big smile on his face. He had scored twelve points! But he never would have scored those points if he hadn't honored his dad's instructions to develop himself. That honor had unlocked his ability and helped him develop a physical gift. Dreams and ambitions are great, but when we link faith to action through honor, we unlock the gifts God has put into our lives.

This is a simple example of how honoring me paid dividends for my son on the basketball court. We'll see this same principle of honor replayed in a spiritual context throughout this book, but the pattern is the same. Honor started with me, the father. I gave my child the provision to play basketball and provided direction and instruction. In return, Jonathan had to honor me to receive a benefit from it.

Honor Brings Unity

As He always has, our heavenly Father constantly extends honor to us, His children. As the father did in the prodigal story, He waits for us to come to our senses and turn to Him. There are so many gifts and abilities He wants to develop in us, but we must honor Him before these things will bear fruit in our lives.

I grew up in church. I tell people I was in church for nine months—three times a week—before I was even born. My dad was a pastor. My grandparents were pastors. I had no choice but to be in church. I heard sermons and more sermons, and many times I responded to what the speakers said. I honored and responded to what they asked me to respond to, and God used those times to change my life.

The honor was extended to me and everyone else listening, but I had to respond to it for God to change my life.

So many people come into the kingdom through a narrow door, then live in the kingdom through a narrow life. After their initial response to the honor God extends to them through Jesus, they stop there. But God has a great deal more for us than the narrow slice of life so many of us experience—more abilities, blessings, and inheritances. He wants us to experience heaven on earth—to live life and to live it abundantly.

He wants you to operate in your gifts and abilities, but honor is the key to releasing these things in your life.

So how does that happen?

The life of honor actually releases you or enables you to access everything the Father has given you. It enables you to unlock the mysteries of the Father. Do you want to see miracles happen in your life? Do you want to see joy, provision, and peace? Look at how God operates—honor is a part of the Trinity in every aspect.

We know that the Godhead is made up of three unique personalities who together reflect the perfection of God. The Father, Son, and Holy Spirit each play a unique role in their interaction with humanity, yet all work in perfect cooperation with each other to achieve the common goal of rescuing, reconciling, and restoring mankind. There is no record of disagreement, disunity, or disharmony in the Godhead—only perfect, pure, and uncompromised unity. This creates an environment for the flow of unimaginable power. Each honors the other equally, and all honor the creation.

THE LIFE OF HONOR ACTUALLY RELEASES YOU OR ENABLES YOU TO ACCESS EVERYTHING THE FATHER HAS GIVEN YOU.

The Bible tells us that God the Father honored the human race by making us a little lower than the angels and crowning us with glory and honor (Hebrews 2:7). He honored us by sending His only Son as a ransom for many (Mark 10:45). The Father also honored Jesus as His beloved Son (John 8:54), who in turn honored the Father by obeying His will (John 8:49; 4:34).

The Holy Spirit then came and honored Jesus by empowering people to continue His ministry (John 16:14–15).

It isn't hard to see a consistent flow of honor between members of the Godhead, as well as an open invitation for all humanity to join that flow as children of God. It's clear that true honor is not limited to upward relationships. God designed it to be practiced between members of the Godhead, between Creator and creation, and between sons and daughters of God who understand and pursue this powerful kingdom principle in their lives.

But our world doesn't celebrate unity or honor toward each other; it celebrates uniqueness, independence, and individuality. God has made each of us unique, but He wants us to use our unique gifts and abilities through a mindset of unity for the sake of the body of Christ.

They say that among humans, 99 percent of our DNA is identical and less than 1 percent is different.[1] We each have different fingerprints and retinas, personalities and talents, vision and taste. What makes us unique is the 1 percent, and what makes us the same is the 99 percent—we're all part of the same body of humanity. God wants us to use our unique gifts and talents, but He wants us to do so through a spirit of unity and for the benefit of the joint body of believers. Just as the Father is different in operation from the Son, and the Son from the Holy Spirit, so are you different from me and your gifts from mine.

---

[1]   http://www.telegraph.co.uk/news/worldnews/northamerica/usa/1416706/DNA-survey-finds-all-humans-are-99.9pc-the-same.html

Paul addressed this need for unity when he said, "And if the ear should say, 'Because I am not an eye, I do not belong to the body,' it would not for that reason stop being part of the body. If the whole body were an eye, where would the sense of hearing be? If the whole body were an ear, where would the sense of smell be? But in fact God has placed the parts in the body, every one of them, just as he wanted them to be" (1 Corinthians 12:16–18).

GOD HAS MADE EACH OF US UNIQUE, BUT HE WANTS US TO USE OUR UNIQUE GIFTS AND ABILITIES THROUGH A MINDSET OF UNITY FOR THE SAKE OF THE BODY OF CHRIST.

In an office, people with different skills must work together to accomplish a project. They must be of one mind. When they all honor the direction of their manager, they can use their uniqueness to produce something greater than any single one of them could alone.

This is similar to the way God wants us to use honor in the body of Christ. But our natural tendency is to think that the kingdom of God is all about our particular gift. Those with the gift of prophecy tend to think it's about the prophetic, and those gifted with mercy think it's all about mercy. But God has given us each of us gifts so we can work together with people who have other gifts. In this way, the body becomes stronger and can accomplish God's purposes here on earth.

We do this when we honor Him and when we honor one another and our respective gifts. As honor is exchanged among the members of the Godhead and between Creator and creation, so we are to honor one another. In so doing, we experience the fulfillment of the gifts He's given to us. But when we don't honor one another and the gifts within us, we can get off course and find ourselves far from home.

"Just Glad You're Home"

When I was a youth leader, I had a young kid in my group named Mark. The first time I met him, he was playing soccer and for some reason he got mad about something that happened in the game and he threw a temper tantrum. We were at youth camp, and he was twelve or so. He wasn't a big kid, but he was fiery. I looked at him and thought, *He's going to be a lot of work!*

As I got to know him better, I learned that he was a good kid who came from a broken, dysfunctional home. Now at the time we had no youth band. I became the youth pastor, and I was the band . . . but that wasn't working.

"Lord, I need a band," I prayed. I felt like He said, "It's in your hand." I didn't understand.

"Where is this band?" I asked.

"There. You see that boy, Mark? He has the desire to be a drummer," the Lord told me.

So I asked Mark, "Do you want to be a drummer?"

"Yeah!" he said. So I encouraged him to take drumming lessons.

God showed me another kid who had the desire to play bass and another who wanted to play the guitar, so I encouraged them to practice and gave the guitarist my guitar. I still needed a keyboardist, and I felt God point me toward this one kid who was always half an hour late to youth meetings. Things had gone really well so far, so I asked him if he played keyboard.

"No, I play drums," he told me. Uh-oh! But then he confessed, "Well, I play a little keyboard." So I talked him into playing keyboard the next week, and you know what? He was a really good keyboard player for a drummer! After that, I was no longer the band.

Over the course of the next four or five years, this band developed and got better and better. Then one day, God told me to start a conference called Planetshakers and to begin with our youth group, which had over a thousand kids—an *enormous* size for Australia, where I pastor.

So we planned a conference, called it Planetshakers, and three hundred kids showed up. But our youth band was the difference maker, and the conference started growing and growing. About 2,500 kids attended each conference, and God touched lives every time.

About that time, Mark told me he couldn't be the drummer that year. He was in jazz college and felt he wanted to pursue other opportunities. Suddenly, I had to find a new drummer— and we were poised to record our first album!

Mark began to play in clubs and to disconnect with the church. He was on the fringes of church life, traveling to Thailand and other Asian countries to play in bands. This was all well and good, but he was no longer a part of our vision. When he was younger, he used to come to our house a lot and eat with us—he ate us out of house and home, even though he was skinny! I'd grown close to this kid, and it broke my heart to see him slipping away from God. But at one point, God told me, "Let him go."

Eventually, God led me to start a church, so after many years in Adelaide, Australia, we moved to Melbourne and launched a church. Not too long after that, Mark turned up at the church. I was friendly with him and loved on him, but he wasn't connected at all.

Then one day he came to me and said, "I need to see you."

"Okay, cool," I told him. So we hopped in the car, because that's where I do my best talking.

Mark turned to me and asked, "Do you think I've been living in deception?"

This surprised me. "What do you mean?" I asked. He explained that though he didn't read much, his mother had gotten him a book by John Bevere called *Under Cover.*

"I read it cover to cover," he told me. "I thought I was doing okay, going my own way. But after I read this book, I realized I had removed myself from cover," he confided.

He finished, "I think I've wasted part of my life."

"Mark," I told him, "only you can know that. But no, I don't think you've been living what you originally talked about." I took my eyes off the road for a moment to drive my point home. "But this is not the end."

It was a powerful moment, and Mark had tears in his eyes. It was even more amazing when our regular drummer, the replacement who had stayed with us for nearly eleven years, had to pull out of our American tour—and Mark took his place. I got to see Mark stand on stage before thousands and thousands of kids and play with Planetshakers. It was as though the intervening years had never happened. God honored him and his gifts through a ministry that has brought thousands to Christ.

I had honored the gifts that God placed inside a skinny, fiery little boy who used to clean out my refrigerator. God had honored those gifts, too; then, like the prodigal son, Mark walked away. But all was not lost—it was not the end.

God is the God of recovery, and He extended honor to Mark even when Mark didn't want to live the dream the Lord had given him as a teen. Mark walked away from what he felt in his heart and ceased to honor the gifts and abilities God had given him. But eleven years later, he acknowledged that he had gone off course.

The last thing I told him in the car was what I think the father said to the prodigal son and what our Father says to us: "I'm just glad you're home."

Mark has served faithfully at our church since then, and he's involved in many ways. He doesn't just use his gifts to play drums; he has grown and serves in other areas, such as on our prayer and production team. God has completely restored him—a powerful example of how God honors us and our gifts and is just waiting for us to honor Him.

The most amazing thing about God's system of honor, the key to bringing the kingdom of heaven to earth, is that it's never too late to learn it and to begin implementing it in your life. You may have lived a dishonoring life, like the prodigal, or have veered off the path of your true dream, like Mark. If you're reading this book and that is true of your life, remember that your story isn't over; the end hasn't been written. You can still be restored and renewed.

Your heavenly Father is just glad you're home.

Thinking as You Ought

The way the Planetshakers band came together demonstrated how honor creates unity within a body. However, pursuing unity over uniqueness goes against our natural inclinations. It goes against the grain of our culture, yet God is calling us to live differently from the world. I asked God how this works, and He began to show me what the restoration of our minds looks like.

THE MOST AMAZING THING ABOUT GOD'S SYSTEM OF HONOR, THE KEY TO BRINGING THE KINGDOM OF HEAVEN TO EARTH, IS THAT IT'S NEVER TOO LATE TO LEARN IT AND TO BEGIN IMPLEMENTING IT IN YOUR LIFE.

Home makeover television shows are really popular in the United States and in Australia. I especially love the ones where the people come back and see the dramatic improvements—the renovated house is far better than the original. That's a great description of what the word *renew* means. God wants to give you a mind that's actually better than the original mind you were born with.

Romans 12:2 says, "Do not conform to the pattern of this world, but be transformed by the renewing of your mind." The term *conform* means "to fashion alike" or "to be in union with." Paul urges us not to think like the world but to be transformed—

the word he uses here is actually the root of *metamorphosis*—by the renewing of our minds.

God wants to host a renovation show, and your mind is the star. The results will be a mind in unity with Him and with the body of Christ, a mind that uses the key of honor to bring the kingdom of God to earth.

Having a mindset of honor moves your thoughts from a focus on yourself and your gifts to those around you. You add your uniqueness to the body, so you're not separate from the community but a vital component in it. When each part honors the other, they're all better together.

Honor is a key component in being transformed by the renewing of our minds, but this requires that we first honor God—and it is this restoration that lets us truly honor one another with more than lip service.

We started this chapter by talking about where honor starts, but I think now is a perfect time to point out that honor doesn't end when we respond in salvation. Honor opens the door to life in Christ, but honor also allows us to live in the fullness God intends for us. Paul makes a strong claim in the second half of the verse in Romans we just read. If we resist being conformed to the pattern of this world and are transformed by the renewing of our minds, "then [we] will be able to test and approve what God's will is—his good, pleasing and perfect will" (Romans 12:2). The reason we don't know God's will in our lives is because we don't have a renewed mind—a mind that honors.

Paul goes on to say, "Do not think of yourself more highly than you ought" (Romans 12:3). This is a difficult concept for me because as a pastor I am training people to believe the best

HAVING A MINDSET OF HONOR MOVES YOUR THOUGHTS FROM A FOCUS ON YOURSELF AND YOUR GIFTS TO THOSE AROUND YOU.

for themselves and to be the best they can be for God. I asked the Lord about this, and His answer revealed how important honor is to the process of mind renewal.

"If they have a renewed mind, people will think rightly of themselves," God told me. When you have a renewed mind, you're no longer thinking more highly than you ought.

"Thinking of yourself more highly than you ought, is doing something you were never called to do," the Lord continued. "It's thinking that your decisions and thoughts are higher than God's."

Transformed thinking is kingdom thinking—it's thinking in one mind with the rest of the body of Christ, in unity and in order, and all underpinned with honor. Each of our gifts brings value and significance to the body. No gift is bigger or smaller— each is integral to the body of Christ.

You Could Shake the Planet

There was a time in my life when fear caused me to think that my decisions and thoughts were higher than God's. I was locked in a cycle of dishonor where I pushed people away with my actions. Thankfully, God used a youth pastor to show me that He never stops offering us honor. He showed me that if we will respond in honor, He can change that cycle of dishonor and bring out the best in us.

Growing up, my youth pastor was a big, emotional Italian guy—he loved everyone, and he cried easily. Although I felt God's call on my life, I had grown up in a relatively well-known Christian family in Australia and I was super insecure because I didn't think I could be like my father. He was my hero and had never, *ever* criticized me. He always loved and supported me, but I believed a lie. I chose to honor a lie rather than the truth of what God had said about me; I believed I would never be able to communicate successfully.

You see, an English teacher in school had told me that I couldn't communicate. She had asked the class to read a book that was objectionable, and my parents had written a note to the school sharing their displeasure with this assignment. This undoubtedly embarrassed her. From that point on, she took out her anger on me, and in my records wrote: "Russell cannot communicate verbally or in writing." Later, the principal removed this comment, but the lie had already been planted in my heart.

So I had the desire to do something great for God and had received many uplifting words from Him about a calling to ministry, but I believed the lie the enemy had planted within me that I couldn't communicate. This conflict produced a critical, abrasive attitude that I took out on those around me.

Once a guest speaker came to preach at my father's church and in a prime example of my miserable attitude at the time I asked, "What great things have you ever done that you should get to preach here?" I asked this right in front of my youth pastor, whose life I had probably just made extremely difficult!

Now, the youth pastor had a choice to make. He could respond with dishonor to this cheeky pastor's kid who mouthed off with embarrassment and rejection to a visiting man of God, or he could pour honor over me that I didn't deserve and pray that I'd respond and receive a renewed mind.

Thankfully, he chose to believe in me.

I clearly remember one evening at a youth camp when I found him crying—he cried a lot, being a very emotional Italian. So I came up to him and asked what was wrong. He replied that nothing was wrong. "Well, why is your head leaking then?" I asked, trying to lighten his mood with one of my standard jokes.

WHEN YOU GIVE OR RELEASE HONOR, YOU ATTRACT HONOR.

He looked at me with tear-reddened eyes and such a moving expression on his face—I couldn't place it at the time. "Because," he told me with this strange ache in his voice, "God is showing me who you *could* be. You could shake the planet."

This youth pastor had every reason to reject me, but he believed in me. He kept loving me, and kept honoring what he could see God wanted to do with my life. Instead of making me want to run away and stay bitter and critical, this made me want to respond to him in a positive way. I didn't know how to explain what was happening then, but I do now: He extended honor to me, and I needed to honor him in return. His action of honor made me *want* to honor him.

Where Honor Starts

So where does honor start? Does it start when you demand it from those under your authority? No.

When you give or release honor, you attract honor. You create a desire in those around you to give honor back. My youth pastor's honor toward me attracted a reciprocal honor from me. He didn't try to manipulate me. He simply believed in me and honored me through his belief.

You may be crying out to God for someone to believe in you like this youth pastor believed in me. What you may not realize is that He has already given you Someone—His name is Jesus.

When there's no other person who believes in you or extends honor to you, know that honor for your life started when God our Father sent His Son to die for you. The Father has never stopped believing in you, never stopped looking for you to turn to Him—not just for salvation but for the abundant kingdom life that is possible when we honor Him in return.

You may not have someone pouring honor into your life, but your heavenly Father never stops releasing honor to you. Your choice to let His honor attract honor within you is the key that will renew your mind and make possible your journey of honor. Honor begins with God, but the key to a life of honor is to respond to Him—every day of your life.

CHAPTER 3

HONOR IS THE FOUNDATION OF THE KINGDOM

Honor is the master key to release the kingdom of heaven and all its fullness in your life. We talked briefly about how this pertains to salvation earlier—you can hear the salvation message over and over again, but until you respond by honoring that good news, you cannot access salvation.

We get into heaven by honoring what Jesus did on the cross, and as we do so, God gives us faith as a free gift. Honor sets us up to receive this gift, but this is just the start of this journey in the kingdom of God.

Jesus taught us to pray for His kingdom to come on earth as it is in heaven, so we know that God's plan is to bring heaven to earth. He wouldn't tell us to pray for it if He knew we couldn't receive it! Heaven is no more sickness or lack; it is abundant joy, peace, and freedom. There are no limits in heaven. That's what the kingdom of heaven is all about.

Jesus told us that everything we saw Him do, He did on behalf of His Father—He gave us a picture of what heaven looks like, in the form of a Man. He also said, "Whoever believes in me will do the works I have been doing, and they will do even greater things than these . . ." (John 14:12).

We are left to wonder how we can do better than raising Lazarus from the dead or healing the woman with the issue of blood who touched the hem of Christ's garment or feeding the five thousand. So let's just clarify for a moment what Jesus meant: He was not saying you'll do "greater" miracles in quality, because there are no greater miracles than those He performed. He was talking about *quantity*.

The Bible says the same Spirit that raised Christ from the dead lives in us, so millions of believers follow Jesus and operate in the power of the Holy Spirit. We have access to the same power that raised Christ from the dead to do miracles here and bring heaven to earth. Through the Spirit, we have the power to heal the sick, raise the dead, cast out devils, and bring freedom and life.

> THROUGH THE SPIRIT, WE HAVE THE POWER TO HEAL THE SICK, RAISE THE DEAD, CAST OUT DEVILS, AND BRING FREEDOM AND LIFE.

The Holy Spirit is heaven's representative on earth. So if you take the Holy Spirit out of the church, you take heaven out of the earth. And what does the Holy Spirit do? He reveals Jesus, who in turn reveals the Father. This is the essence of how honor works within the Trinity.

This is precisely the way honor works within our lives and why it's the key to release the kingdom of heaven and all its fullness in your life. It's important for every Christian to understand this, because if you understand honor you will pursue it. And in giving honor, you will attract honor.

Honor Opens the Door to Miracles

As I look at Jesus' life, every miracle and breakthrough came when honor was present.

In Jesus' first miracle He turned water into wine. No one knew Him; He was just a simple carpenter attending a wedding when something went wrong. His mother said, "You need to fix the situation." This "disaster" was actually a perfect picture of dishonor—midway through the celebration the wedding host ran out of wine, which would have brought shame to the family.

So Mary turned to Jesus in a situation where there was dishonor and shame and told Him that He needed to fix it. His answer is priceless: "Woman . . . my hour has not yet come" (John 2:4). If I had said that to my mom, I would have felt the aftereffects into the next week!

But Mary ignored His response and instructed the servants to do whatever He told them to do. In that moment, Jesus had to choose whether to honor His mother or not. What followed is an extreme example of the power of honor to change an earthly situation with the power of heaven. The servants had to honor Mary and then honor Jesus' instructions—they had to carry what they thought to be *water* to the master of ceremonies!

> WHEN WE HONOR
> HIS INSTRUCTIONS,
> WE EXCHANGE
> DISHONOR, SHAME,
> AND THE BAD
> THINGS IN OUR
> LIVES FOR THE JOYS
> AND BLESSINGS OF
> THE FATHER.

He tasted it and praised it as being the best wine served that day. Jesus had just performed His first miracle.

Jesus transformed the dishonor of that moment into an incredible example of how the Father pours honor into a situation and brings the power of heaven to earth. It was actually a prophetic moment, too, because it declared what Jesus was going to do in His ministry: take the natural and make it supernatural. He showed us that when we honor His instructions, we exchange dishonor, shame, and the bad things in our lives for the joys and blessings of the Father. It was a tiny taste of breakthrough where there had been bondage, and joy where there had been sorrow.

This miracle was the foundation of every miracle Jesus performed.

We see the stark contrast to this miracle when Jesus returned to His hometown later in His ministry. He knew all the troubles of the people in His hometown—who had been sick for a long time or in bondage to the devil and so much more. He probably couldn't wait to bring the blessings and power of the kingdom of heaven to the people He had known His whole life.

He had done mighty miracles throughout Judea, but in His hometown they said, "Who is this? He's just the carpenter's boy." Familiarity had bred contempt, and they didn't honor the power of God on His life. And because they didn't honor Him, they couldn't receive what He had to bring.

They didn't use the key to unlock their breakthrough and miracles. Because they didn't honor the power of God in Jesus, they didn't believe. "And because of their unbelief, he couldn't do any miracles . . . " (Mark 6:5 NLT).

HONOR IS THE FOUNDATION OF THE KINGDOM, AND IT UNLOCKS THE POSSIBILITIES OF HEAVEN.

I guarantee that Jesus wanted to do so much more for the people He had grown up with. He knew exactly what they needed, but He couldn't deliver supernatural solutions because they didn't honor what He wanted to do.

Honor is the foundation of the kingdom, and it unlocks the possibilities of heaven.

Taking Fire to the Nations

Perhaps you think that if Jesus had come from *your* hometown, you would have honored and received from Him. It's easy to think that. The problem is, all too often the evidence is to the contrary. We may not think we would reject Him if He showed up to visit, but we can believe that our decision-making is higher than God's. In so doing, we don't think correctly about ourselves.

I shared with you the gist of my own youthful insecurities and how they temporarily prevented me from honoring God's words to me and His desires to work through me. But let me tell you about a time when I honored a most unusual directive from God—and received the seed of a greater inheritance than I could have dreamed possible.

It happened while I was attending a large conference. At the time, no thought of Planetshakers had yet entered my mind. I had the desire to change the world, but it was just an abstract desire. At this meeting, the Holy Spirit moved in some unusual ways, and while some people criticized what was going on, others were touched by God in unique and amazing ways.

I was on the front row with my wife, surrounded by about ten thousand people. Suddenly I felt the Spirit of God urge me to respond to Him in a way I never had before. *There's no way I'm going to do that,* was my initial thought, but this urge increased. I resisted—I kept seeing the faces and hearing the voices of the critics. I squeezed my eyes closed and kept a death grip on my chair. I didn't want to honor this urge of the Spirit.

Suddenly the preacher said something loudly, and it startled me. Before I knew what I was doing, I acted on the urge the Spirit had placed upon me. I kept asking myself, "Why am I doing this?" especially as I didn't feel a great, weighty presence of the Lord. At the time, many people saw me worship God in a way I had never worshipped before. Everyone at the conference could see me. My actions were unorthodox and out of my comfort zone. But they were a response that honored what the Lord had urged me to do.

After the service, three people lined up to talk to me— all were big critics of the way the Spirit had been moving in the conference. The first came up to me and said, "You looked stupid." In my head, I couldn't help but agree. "That was a crazy thing to do," said the next person, and the third echoed that.

Then I turned to see someone I didn't know standing behind me. He'd seen me, too. "Russell, I know you don't know me. I was sitting up in the bleachers," he said. "God gave me a vision—a picture of you taking fire to the nations."

A few moments later, another person wanted to talk as well. "I was sitting in the middle of the stadium, and God showed me something for you—you were taking fire to the nations." A third person came up to me: "I was sitting in the third row, and I saw you. When you did that, God gave me a picture in my head of you taking fire to the nations." A fourth said nearly the same thing—all had come from different parts of the building, didn't know each other or me, and yet received the same vision from the Lord.

I had stepped out as God had urged me to—what I call the Bartimaeus response. God took my desire to change the world and planted a seed that day: He would use me to take His presence to the nations.

The Bartimaeus Response

God can urge us to respond, but ultimately the choice to honor Him or not is ours. I think of blind Bartimaeus sitting on the roadside. He had a desire from God—to be healed. He had that urge, and it was from the Lord.

He responded to it by crying out, "Jesus, Son of David, have mercy on me!" (Mark 10:47). Those around him told him to be quiet, but it didn't deter him—he shouted all the more. Then Jesus called to him, and Bartimaeus responded immediately: "Throwing his cloak aside, he jumped to his feet and came to Jesus" (Mark 10:50).

Jesus asked him to put himself in an extremely vulnerable situation—to step forward and come to Jesus. Remember, he was blind; stepping forward wasn't likely to be gracious and could easily make him look foolish. But he didn't just step—he threw off his beggar's coat, which represented who he was, and he *leapt!* And what was he leaping to? A voice, a call. What was he doing? He was honoring God's voice.

ANY MOVE OF THE KINGDOM OF GOD REQUIRES THAT WE RESPOND TO HIS VOICE WITH HONOR.

We all want God to do things in our lives, but any move of the kingdom of God requires that we respond to His voice with honor. A response to God's voice often has the potential of making us look foolish to human eyes, but responding in honor is the key that unlocks the blessings God wants to bestow on us.

In my life, I wanted God to use me to take His presence to the nations, but I didn't know how. I wanted a vision.

What I received was a call.

It Started with Honor

At a meeting a year later, I had another encounter with God where He actually called me to do two things. First, God said to me, "Start a conference called Planetshakers."

I responded with the highly spiritual answer of, "What's that?" God responded with an even more spiritual answer: "Just do it." This was a call, a voice like the one blind Bartimaeus heard, and I had to choose whether to respond with honor—or not.

Immediately after telling me to start Planetshakers, the Lord said, "Have the young people take up a firstfruits offering." Again, I asked Him what that was—I had never heard of it. "Ask them to give a whole week's wage," the Lord answered.

"Lord," I responded like a true man of God, "I like people *liking* me. I'm not going to ask them to give a week's wages in an offering—they'll hate me!"

"Do it," the Lord replied. "Tell them the offering will go to seed Planetshakers (one third), to missions (one third), and to local evangelism (one third)." He was calling me to step out, potentially looking foolish to others, in order to honor the call He had given me.

So I said, "Okay." I went back to our youth and said, after a deep breath, "We're going to take up a firstfruits offering—a week's wage. It will be used to start a conference called Planetshakers, and we'll use it to make registrations really cheap—this seed offering will pay for students. I want to teach a generation to give, not pay."

Thankfully, they didn't stone me. In fact, these amazing young people gave $66,000! Twenty-two thousand went to fund the conference, the next third went to evangelism, and the final third funded a project in a needy area of our town.

Three hundred kids attended our first conference, and the registration was only ten dollars each because of the seed offering. I honored God's word to me, and years later, *millions* of people around the world have heard Planetshakers' music and sing the songs, we have a thriving church born from the ministry, and we have conferences with thirty thousand in attendance.

Truly God has used a small step of honor—my obedience to Him despite the risk of looking foolish—to bring about a great inheritance that has blessed countless people around the world.

And it started with honor.

Obedience Is Success

I like to say that Noah is the second greatest leader of all time. When people ask me how I've come to that conclusion, I answer that Jesus was the greatest because He saved us from our sins, but without Noah there would be no one to save. You could say that honor saved the world!

The thing about Noah that blows me away is that he honored God *for 120 years*. See, it's good to honor God for a day. It's good to honor Him for a week, or a month. But imagine honoring God for 120 years without seeing any evidence that what you're doing is working!

We want instant results from honoring God. We want to see that our efforts result in immediate success. Yet whether or not you think your decision to honor is "working" has *everything* to do with how you judge success. So what is true success?

The answer is obedience. Obedience is success. When you honor God with your obedience . . . that is success. Faithfulness will follow.

Joshua is another great example of this truth. He honored God's promise for forty years in the wilderness. The long delay was not because he lacked honor, but because the people he was leading lacked honor. Yet for all the time he spent in the wilderness, Joshua didn't let the wilderness affect him. He continued to honor the promise that he and the children of Israel would enter the Promised Land.

WHEN YOU HONOR GOD WITH YOUR OBEDIENCE . . . THAT IS SUCCESS. FAITHFULNESS WILL FOLLOW.

Though it took 120 years, God saved all humanity through Noah because he persevered in honor. Though it took forty years, God gave the land to the children of Israel under Joshua's leadership. Honor was the key that unlocked these inheritances, and it is the key to unlock the inheritance God has for you. But when it comes down to it, obedience must be your measure of success.

The Culture of the Kingdom

A kingdom is the dominion of a king—it reflects the characteristics of the king. So if the king is love, the characteristic of his kingdom will be love. One of the key characteristics of our King is honor. So when we honor God's voice or work in our lives, we respond in harmony with a characteristic of His kingdom. The nature of God's character is honor, the nature of His kingdom is honor, and a key to His kingdom is honor.

So how do you gain more of these characteristics? You must get more of the King in your life. The more time you spend with Him, the more you'll be like Him. You must be in one mind with Him, in unity. And that requires a transformation of your mind.

You received a free gift when you honored the message of salvation and responded, and that began a supernatural process to become more and more like God's Son. As we walk with God, He begins to renew our minds, to give us the mind of Christ. We increase this process when we create an environment where these godly characteristics can flourish.

This environment is a culture of honor. What is a culture? It's an environment that causes growth. Think of a greenhouse—plants that develop in a culture of growth, rich in warmth and nutrients, are not subject to the hostile elements that exist outside of that environment. They are subject only to the environment or culture inside the greenhouse.

We have a choice between two cultures: that of the flesh or that of the spirit—that of the world or of the kingdom of God. Because the King's characteristic is honor, the culture of His kingdom is honor.

YOU HONOR WHAT YOU WALK TOWARD.

Your flesh doesn't want to honor. To the flesh, it's foolish. Your spirit does want to honor, and so you must answer the question: "Which is the real you?" How will you choose? Your spirit will live for eternity, but your flesh will rot in the ground. So which will you choose? Which will create the culture for your life?

Since our spirits will live forever in the kingdom of heaven, it seems to me that we should refuse to honor the flesh and should choose instead to honor the kingdom of the Spirit. *This* is choosing your new mind. It's a choice that will impact the entire culture and environment of your life. You will live in a culture of honor.

You Honor What You Walk Toward

To change the atmosphere of your life, you must be like the King of the kingdom you seek to honor. Elements such as worship, reading the Word, and being in God's presence shift the environment of your life toward a culture of honor. When you give God the first of your day, the first of your money, and the first of your obedience, you honor Him. When the youth I ministered to did this, Planetshakers was born. What will God do through you? It depends on what you're headed toward.

I like to say it like this: You honor what you walk toward. When you walk toward the priorities of the flesh, toward insecurities or lies that keep you bound, you honor the wrong culture. When you walk toward the priorities of the Spirit, you honor the culture of the kingdom of heaven.

When you spend time with your Father instead of with your problems, you step toward Him just as Bartimeus did when he stumbled toward Jesus. After all, Jesus didn't teach us to pray "Our problems here on earth . . ."; He taught us to pray, "Our Father which art in heaven, hallowed be thy name" (Matthew 6:9 KJV).

Hallowed isn't a word we use much anymore, but it's a word of honor. It means to honor something, to hold it in the highest possible esteem. Jesus taught us to start by honoring the Father, because when we honor our problems, all we think about are our problems. But when we start with honoring the Father, we set the culture of our lives to be an environment that promotes growth.

Want to change your culture? Want to renew your mind? Start by honoring your Father. Hallowed is His name, for He is mighty, awesome, and worthy of praise! When you do this, you not only honor your Father, you also honor the position you have in His kingdom as His son or daughter. This is how to have a heavenly viewpoint. It's the key to release the kingdom of God in your life.

CHAPTER 4

HONOR IS THE OPPOSITE OF CONTROL

Many people have an incorrect view of honor because the term has been abused or misused. Some have shared with me that they resist the concept of honor because they see it as an excuse for someone in authority to try to control them and use it as leverage.

The reality is that honor is the *opposite* of control. Let's look into the life of the prodigal son again and see how his father responded to him. Did the father try to control the son? Jesus gave this parable to us as an example, so let's see what it shows us about honor.

I believe it's clear that when the prodigal came home, his father didn't try to control him. What did the father do? He poured honor out on the son—he put a coat over his rags, sandals on his dirty feet, and a ring on his naked finger. Without hesitation, the father restored him to sonship, with all the rights and privileges that came with being his son. This restoration and celebration bears no resemblance to an effort to control.

So if the father didn't try to control, and this is a representation of our heavenly Father, what does it say about Him and His culture of honor? It tells me that the nature of honor is not control—nothing the prodigal's father did was controlling. Honor is the vehicle through which God pours out blessings and inheritance upon us, just as the father did on the prodigal.

So what happens when there is no honor?

What Fills the Honor Void?

I've noticed that when there's a lack of honor, something else takes its place to make things happen. Honor is the key that unlocks the inheritance God wants to give us, but when it isn't present, a counterfeit tries to fill that void. The most common counterfeits for honor are control, manipulation, and intimidation.

We see examples of these counterfeits in the story of the prodigal son when the elder brother came in from the field to find the celebration party in full swing.

> The older brother became angry and refused to go in. So his father went out and pleaded with him. But he answered his father, 'Look! All these years I've been slaving for you and never disobeyed your

orders. Yet you never gave me even a young goat so I could celebrate with my friends. But when this son of yours who has squandered your property with prostitutes comes home, you kill the fattened calf for him! (Luke 15:28–30)

From his early statements, you might think that the elder son truly honored the father—he had worked in the fields and obeyed his whole life. But listen to the buttons he pushes with his little rant. I especially love his choice of words when he says, "This son of *yours*"!

Now notice the father's reply: "'My son,' the father said, 'you are always with me, and everything I have is yours. But we had to celebrate and be glad, because this brother of yours was dead and is alive again; he was lost and is found'" (Luke 15:31–32). I love how the father not only extended honor toward this elder son but turned the language around on him and said "This brother of *yours*."

If the elder son had had an honoring heart like his father, he would have seized the opportunity to extend honor toward his brother. He could have made that choice, but instead, he opted to control and to manipulate the honoring father.

> I'VE NOTICED THAT WHEN THERE'S A LACK OF HONOR, SOMETHING ELSE TAKES ITS PLACE TO MAKE THINGS HAPPEN.

Many of us have grown up learning to control, manipulate, and intimidate others to achieve our own desires. We watched others get what they wanted that way, and it appealed to our unredeemed nature. It's common to see parents use control, manipulation, and intimidation to get their children to behave. (I confess I've done it myself, but more on that in a moment.) It should be no surprise that children then emulate their counterfeiting parents.

We hear parents order their children about, and we wonder why those children are little controlling tyrants on the playground. We hear parents bribe with a treat if the child will behave in the store and wonder why the same child manipulates to get what he wants. We hear parents threaten their kids, and we wonder why those kids bully and intimidate. They've been raised in a counterfeit culture instead of an atmosphere of honor.

Now, is a family of honor a family of sloppy grace, where the kids get to do whatever they want? Actually, I believe that a family of honor will embrace correction—not just for the parents, but for the children.

A good friend of mine maintains that when he corrects his children, the appropriate response should be, "Thank you for correcting me and making me a better person, Dad." This is significant because it reinforces to the child that making them "better" or more mature is the ultimate goal and heart behind all the correction. And that is at the heart of honor. On the other hand, correction applied with an attitude of control, manipulation, and intimidation is out of order.

Honor Is About "Our"

In a world that's focused on individuals, it's all about *my* rights, *my* gifts, and doing *my* thing. And in order to get my way, I control, manipulate, and intimidate. However, honor is about *us* and *our,* not *me* and *my.* In America, the spelling of "honor" has lost something important— the "u." In England and Australia, it's spelled *honour* because God wants to

> **HONOR IS ABOUT US *AND* OUR, NOT ME *AND* MY.**

honor "u" so you'll make *honour* about *"our."* It isn't about my rights or gifts, it's about *our* blessings as the body of Christ— about things that are for *our* good. The same is true for favor— God wants to make it *our* fav*our* as a body, not *my* favor as an individual.

When you honor, you are looked after—and so is everyone else. This is a kingdom culture that's unique to those who honor. It's a kingdom of community, for the kingdom is about "us." Note the beginning of the Lord's Prayer: *"Our* Father in heaven," not *"My* Father in heaven."

The very essence of God is *our*—the Father, Son, and Holy Spirit are a community of three in one. Remember, a kingdom is like its king, and God thinks in terms of community, unity, and of the body as a whole.

Honor is the opposite of control, because control is all about *me,* and honor is all about *us.* The reason most people leave churches (or other group activities) is because they decide that it's not meeting their needs in some way. Marriages break down because spouses move away from being about *us* to being about *me.* The relationship becomes about *my* needs, and in order to get *my* needs met, I resort to control, manipulation, and intimidation.

Sometimes we manipulate, but we do it in a nice way. In our home, we've tried to cultivate a culture of honor, but one time I spoke to my daughter, Aimee, and said, half-joking, "If you really loved me, you'd do this for me." Because we honor each other in our home, my daughter, at thirteen years of age, came back and said, "Dad, you're using manipulation, and you can't do that in this family!"

I had to laugh about it, and her mother was in the corner with a smile on her face just looking at me. What Aimee said was true: I had used manipulation to get what I wanted instead of creating an environment of honor.

Just recently my wife, Sam, was away on a ministry trip, and Aimee cooked all the meals—brilliant meals every day. When I asked Aimee why she wanted to do that, she said, "Mom's away, Dad, so I need to look after you and make sure you don't eat badly." She honored her mother by making sure I had the same healthy options available to me that Sam would have provided. She honored me by wanting to look after me.

Her actions and attitudes were focused on *us*. Had she been focused on herself, she might have chosen not to be inconvenienced or to do something for someone else. When we try to get something based on our tendencies to be independent, we have to intimidate, manipulate, and control, but when honor is released, it's all about *us*.

We Honor as Heirs of God

It can be easy to honor our leaders when we understand where we are in relation with them and are the recipients of their acts of service in our lives. Likewise, it is fairly easy to honor people we want to help or serve. It can be really difficult, however, to honor our peers.

Honor releases the gift you carry because it releases the inheritance God wants to give others through you. So when I honor someone who is going through a difficult experience because they need to be lifted up, I emulate Jesus and the Father. Jesus honored His Father by coming to earth to die, but He also honored us when we were still sinners, lost and on our way to hell.

SO WHEN I HONOR SOMEONE WHO IS GOING THROUGH A DIFFICULT EXPERIENCE BECAUSE THEY NEED TO BE LIFTED UP, I EMULATE JESUS AND THE FATHER.

So what did He do? He reached down into our lives, lifted us out of our spiritual death by uniting us with Jesus (Ephesians 2:6), and raised us up to be seated with Christ in heavenly places. He honored us by making us His sons and daughters and positioning us alongside His Son, Jesus, as peers. Jesus was the firstborn from the dead, the firstborn Son of God, but we are adopted into His family and can cry out Abba, Father because He honored us. He made us heirs of His promise.

So many people still have an orphan's heart instead of the heart of God's son or daughter. We were slaves, and we think we are still unworthy. So, like an orphan, we resort to what we know—we control, manipulate, and intimidate to meet our needs. When we do this we show that we haven't received a revelation of our position as co-heirs with Christ (Romans 8:15–17).

Or we may grow too familiar with the Father and take our position for granted. There's a difference between familiarity and intimacy. Familiarity breeds contempt, but intimacy promotes a deepening relationship. The difference is honor. Familiarity is lip service—we can say all the right things—but honor backs up words with actions. When we honor the Lord, we grow in intimacy with Him as His sons and daughters.

Honor Gives to Give

Honor doesn't give to get; honor gives to give. Some people give with a sow-and-reap mentality. They don't give to be generous; they give because they're selfish and want to get more. Honor doesn't do this—it gives generously because this shows honor. Now, it's true that we always reap when we sow, but that's not the purpose of giving—that's just a fortunate byproduct!

When people get upset because they show honor but don't receive honor in return, it shows they are simply giving to get something back. This is actually a form of manipulation or control. When we truly honor others, we don't look for anything in return—we simply honor them because that's our culture, the nature of the kingdom to which we belong.

WHEN WE TRULY HONOR OTHERS, WE DON'T LOOK FOR ANYTHING IN RETURN.

Jesus doesn't come to us and say, "Look, I've done this for you, but you haven't done this back." He says, "This is what I've done for you. Come receive your inheritance!"

When "Pharisees" urge us to do something in order to get something, under the guise of honor, they promote religion . . . not relationship. Control always expects something in return, but honor doesn't expect anything—it just wants to release and give.

So many times I've heard people say, "I'm not going to honor anymore, because I honored this person and he didn't honor me back." What they don't realize is that their "orphan heart" was manipulating and was not honoring at all. They were giving to get, not giving to release something.

If you can grasp this difference, it will be a paradigm shift in how you view honor and how you experience the inheritance that comes with it.

Warning: Contents Under Pressure

The pressures of life really determine our willingness to show honor. When everything is going great, people will readily say things like, "It's an honor to be part of this," or, "We're honored to serve." But if pressure comes or perception changes—if someone does something they don't agree with—it can be a game changer. How about you? Will you continue to honor when things become difficult?

Simon Peter shifted in and out of honor. He denied Christ three times when the pressure came, and this was the same man who had the revelation that Jesus was the Christ, the Son of the living God. If Jesus' goal in rising from the dead had been to receive honor, He wouldn't have kept honoring Peter. The man wasn't even at the tomb, though for three years of discipleship

HONOR WILL BELIEVE IN THE GREATNESS GOD HAS PUT IN A PERSON, EVEN WHEN THAT PERSON HAS YET TO RETURN HONOR AND BE WORTHY OF THAT FAITH.

ministry Jesus had said He would rise again! Simon Peter was hiding. Yet after Jesus rose from the dead, He reached out to Peter and prepared a special breakfast on the seashore to honor him (John 21).

And what person did Jesus use to start the church? Peter. Jesus honored him repeatedly; Peter was the rock on which Jesus chose to build His church. *That* is the nature of honor, and Jesus understood it intimately because the Godhead has been honoring since before time began.

Jesus continued to believe in Peter, to honor him and the gift God had put in him. Honor will believe in the greatness God has put in a person, even when that person has yet to return honor and be worthy of that faith. Our faith isn't in the person; our faith is in God. But honor is what brings the gift forth as we release it into someone's life.

So many people have said to me, "I'll be with you until the day I die"—and then they've left. Other people have messed up in one way or another and have hurt me. I've had to make a choice: become cynical and not trust people or keep believing, trusting, and honoring. That's what my youth pastor did—he kept believing in me. That's what Jesus did for Peter—He kept believing in him.

Control seeks to restrict; honor seeks to release. God continued to honor and release to us, even when we rejected Him. He never seeks to control us, He only honors us.

Honor Reciprocated

We release something amazing when we choose to honor.

Now, you can choose to honor your parents though they may never honor you in return. This is better than showing no honor at all, because you're not honoring in order to *get,* you're honoring to *release.*

But something else happens when honor is reciprocated. As with us, Peter had to eventually respond with honor to receive the inheritance God wished to give him. That reciprocated honor gave birth to Jesus' bride, the church here on earth.

Peter gave honor to Jesus when he recognized Him as the Son of God, but pressure brought his true nature to the surface—he still had an orphan's heart. Later, Peter's presence in the upper room at Pentecost showed that he had ascribed to a culture of honor. Even under the pressure from the Jews, he received the Holy Spirit and stood up to testify boldly that Jesus was the Son of God to the very crowd that had crucified Christ.

Jesus had honored Peter for three years, but when Peter reciprocated and gave honor back to Him, something amazing happened. Even under persecution, the church received an inheritance and experienced phenomenal growth under the gift of Peter's leadership.

Jesus believed in that gift when Peter evidenced no response. Jesus didn't attempt to control him—He kept on believing, even when pressure revealed that Peter wasn't ready. And Jesus continued to believe in him as Peter reciprocated, which released the inheritance that birthed the church.

That brings up the question, what inheritance will the Lord bring into your life as you respond to His honor? God doesn't want to control you; He believes in you and looks forward to the day when you will reciprocate that honor so He can pour an inheritance into your life!

Honor is the opposite of control, for He doesn't seek something for Himself. God seeks to use honor to bless *you*.

APPOINTED

How can I lay down a lifestyle of manipulation, intimidation, and control and pick up a lifestyle of honor?

You might be thinking, "How hard will this be? What systems and rules can I put in place to ensure I honor others rather than control and manipulate them to get my own way?" Unfortunately, not only can we have misconceptions about the term *honor*, we can also have misconceptions about a lifestyle of honor.

I come again to the parable of the prodigal to illustrate what we must do in order to begin a lifestyle of honor. It's not complicated but is simple, clear, and transforming.

In one word . . . *repent.*

Regarding the prodigal son, Jesus said that "When he came to his senses, he said, 'How many of my father's hired servants have food to spare, and here I am starving to death!'. . . So he got up and went to his father." (Luke 15:17, 20). This is the very definition of repentance.

What must you do in order to enter into a lifestyle of honor? Tell the Lord you're sorry—tell Him that sometimes you manipulate and control and intimidate without even knowing it, but you'd like to stop. Come to your senses, acknowledge your sin, and turn away from it.

We expect to jump through hoops. We want to make it complicated, with Ten Commandments for Living a Life of Honor. But honor has nothing to do with the law and everything to do with *grace*.

> HONOR HAS NOTHING TO DO WITH THE LAW AND EVERYTHING TO DO WITH GRACE.

We may think honor is about works, similar to people who come to God for the first time and want to make the process all about rules— what they can and cannot do. They think they have to get all cleaned up in order to come to Jesus or they have to follow certain codes of conduct or do certain things to earn His favor. People can think of honor in these terms as well.

The thing is, honor isn't earned. It's appointed. It's like grace.

Become Intimate with God

When you get saved and receive Jesus' Spirit within you, His grace begins to change your nature. This happens from the inside out. You can be from the roughest walk of life, but when

Jesus gets a hold of you, things begin to change on the inside. It may happen suddenly, but more often than not, it's a gradual process. You begin to lose interest in some of the things you did previously, and you no longer want to do them. They no longer give you joy or make you feel good. They trigger something in your spirit that feels uncomfortable (conviction), and step by step you and the Lord work out your salvation with fear and trembling.

When you decide to live a lifestyle of honor and begin to reciprocate the honor that God has extended to you, the same type of spiritual transformation works in you to make the control, manipulation, and intimidation that once felt natural now feel unfulfilling and distasteful. Once you sample true honor and the power and blessing that God brings into your life through it, you'll no longer want the counterfeit. The taste of the real thing spoils you for anything else.

Repentance and honor allow God to pour His blessings on you, just as the honoring father did to his prodigal son. He returned his son to his appointed place with a robe on his shoulders, a ring on his finger, and sandals on his feet.

> WE DON'T HONOR TO GET, WE HONOR IN ORDER TO RELEASE.

When you start to honor, you embrace the process of renewing your mind, and spiritually speaking, God does within you what the father did for the prodigal.

I like to say it like this: what you become intimate with, you produce. It's a natural process of grace and renewal; it's not about your works. We don't honor to get, we honor in order to release, and in the truest expression of God's grace, reciprocating honor releases the blessings of God into your life.

This connection between grace and honor is important because if you get off-target into works, this hinders what God wants to do through you. It's also vital because not only are you appointed as a son or daughter of God who receives the free gift of His honor, but He turns this principle on its head and appoints people for you to honor in turn. If you approach it with works, you'll honor others to get. Only the power of grace allows you to honor in order to release and to stay in the right perspective.

Who Is Appointed In Your Life?

Paul says in Romans 13:1, "Everyone must submit to governing authorities. For all authority comes from God, and those in positions of authority have been placed there by God" (NLT). The next verse is even harder to accept: "Therefore whoever resists the authority resists the ordinance of God, and those who resist will bring judgment on themselves" (Romans 13:2 NKJV). Paul then wraps up this little beauty by saying that we are to render honor to everyone to whom it is due, even those placed over us by God.

The principle here is that you didn't appoint your parents, God did. And He tells you in Scripture to honor them. They're your parents—they don't have to earn your honor, they're your parents. Your boss doesn't have to earn your honor; your boss is over you. Your pastor is over you. (With these last two, if you don't want to honor them you can get another job or find another church, but as long as you're there, you should be subject to them and give them honor.)

See, what we often say is, "I'll honor him because I like him," or, "I'll honor my boss when she treats me the way I deserve to be treated." That's not honor, that's *like*. All too often, we confuse *honor* and *respect,* which I'll get into a little later.

> WHEN GOD APPOINTS PEOPLE IN OUR LIVES— HE DOES THE APPOINTING, NOT US—WE ARE SIMPLY TO HONOR THEM.

When God appoints people in our lives—He does the appointing, not us—we are simply to honor them. They may treat us poorly or may not seem worthy of our respect, but that's not the issue. If we want to wait to give honor until the world treats us the way we want, we might as well go back to our mothers' wombs, because the moment we're born someone slaps us!

Life is full of hurt and pain, inflicted by those in authority over us as well as by our peers and others. If pain is the reason we don't honor, we might as well stop living, because anyone can hurt us and not treat us as we would like. We must drop the idea that we'll honor what we like and accept the Word's instruction to honor those whom God has appointed over us.

Can you see how living under grace is so important in the light of this command to respect those appointed over us? We honor others, not because they treat us well but because we belong to God's kingdom. Honor is not about what we receive, honor is about what we release.

This can be a difficult concept to wrestle with because we've all had people in our lives who were difficult to honor. And yet, God appointed these people in a position of authority over us. Why?

I mentioned earlier the English teacher who said I couldn't communicate. Despite disagreeing with her and the book she wanted us to read, my parents taught me that even if she treated me poorly, I was to honor her.

Another time, I was at a pre-service prayer meeting with the worship team when the church's creative director saw me looking out the window. I didn't think I was doing anything wrong, but with my parents away on a ministry trip, he sat me down and told me I had an attitude problem and needed to take a three-month "break" from the worship team. At that same time, I had an offer to play music in bars and clubs, so I felt as though the church was rejecting me while the world was offering me opportunities.

> HE MAY NOT CHANGE OUR CIRCUMSTANCES, BUT HE WILL ALWAYS WALK WITH US THROUGH THEM.

My first words when my parents returned from their trip were, "I'm leaving the church." My dad asked why, and I told him the whole story.

He sat me down and told me, "Russell, things happen in this life that we don't understand. You can't ask, 'Why is this happening' or, 'Why did that happen?'" Then he said, "What you can do is honor God and those He places over you."

My father didn't reverse the creative director's decision; *he walked me through it.* He had the power to change it, but he taught me to honor others even when things didn't go right for me.

God is like this as well. He is all-powerful, but He is not as interested in our convenience as He is in our character. He may not change our circumstances, but He will always walk with us *through* them.

Wisdom and Discernment

I need to emphasize again that we honor under the mandate of grace, not the law. I say this again because someone may read that God calls us to honor those appointed over us and have some circumstances that are not simply unpleasant but completely misdirected.

I told you about the offer I had to play music in bars and clubs at the time I felt rejected by the church. Well, that offer came from a teacher. If you don't understand the proper concept of authority, you might think that because he was appointed over me as a teacher, I could have "honored" him by playing music in the world.

To shed some light on this, let me say two things. First, it's important to note that those appointed over us have a limit to their scope of authority. A teacher has authority in matters pertaining to school. This teacher had no authority over my life outside of school. You would honor your boss and what he expects of you as it pertains to work, but if it interferes with aspects of your life outside of work, you are going to have to use discernment. People appointed over us have a scope of authority.

Second, we must ask God for wisdom and discernment because some people over us are abusive, not just hard to like. A woman may read in the Bible that she is to submit to her husband and then read that she is to honor those appointed over her and think that she should stay near a man who beats her and threatens her life. But she is not obligated to honor any abusive authority. The teacher who invited me to play in bars was inviting me to participate in something I felt was sin—I would have to pretend to be of age among other problems. If honoring someone would place you in danger or cause you to sin, you must ask the Holy Spirit for wisdom and discernment about honor in that situation. You may have to do so from a distance, and you may have to keep in mind that your situation is unique. Honor in your life doesn't necessarily look like honor in someone else's life.

When people don't practice authority as appointed by God, or when you must go against God's Word to honor them, you have no obligation to honor that appointment.

Honor, Respect, and Relationships

I want to take a moment to go back to the idea that honor and respect are not the same, though we sometimes mistakenly interchange these words. Respect is earned. Honor is appointed. I can respect people because of what they have done or what they stand for; I honor people because of their position.

A great example is our political leaders. You may not be able to respect your president because you disagree with his decisions or his ideology. However, because you're a citizen, you must honor his position.

Honor is a vehicle God uses to take you to a destination. It's a

RESPECT IS EARNED. HONOR IS APPOINTED.

kingdom key to move you to kingdom living, and if you don't have it, your progress will be hindered. There are fewer places where this is more clear than in the home.

Peter charges, "In the same way, you husbands must give honor to your wives. Treat your wife with understanding as you live together. She may be weaker than you are, but she is your equal partner in God's gift of new life. Treat her as you should so your prayers will not be hindered" (I Peter 3:7 NLT).

As we'll explore later, God is into order—and God has placed an order in our homes. Husbands and wives are to submit to one another and become "heirs together," as another translation says. The clear connection here is that there's a problem if we don't honor—we'll be hindered.

The writer of Ephesians tells us that we are to submit to one another in marriage, and that wives are to respect their husbands as they would Jesus. Husbands in turn are to love their wives sacrificially, as Christ loves the church (Ephesians 5:21–27).

So who does what first? We all think that if the husband loves the wife, then she will submit. Or if the wife respects the husband, he will love her. Actually, it's a bit of a trick question—husbands and wives are to honor one another regardless of what the other does. (But if you really want to press the point, recall that honor starts with the Father, so the husband should

OUR RELATIONSHIP WITH GOD WAS RESTORED WITH HONOR, AND HONOR IS THE SYSTEM GOD HAS BUILT FOR BLESSING OUR RELATIONSHIPS WITH HIM AND OTHERS.

establish the honor and order of his house. That being said, his failure to do so doesn't excuse his wife from showing him honor.)

Honoring can be hard in a difficult marriage, but before you start explaining why you can't honor your spouse because of the way he or she behaves, reaffirm to yourself that you will honor regardless of what you get out of it. Your husband or wife is appointed to your life in a partnership, and partnerships run on honor. The essential essence to grasp is that honor doesn't look for anything in return—we honor because we're children of God. We honor with no strings attached.

Remember, honor is about *our,* not *me* or *my.* God's is not a kingdom of self but a kingdom of family. We don't honor to receive for ourselves, we honor because we want our entire family to receive God's inheritance. Honor is the vehicle for the fortunate by-product of receiving.

Do you know that God received something when He honored us? Think about that for a moment—*God received something back* when He honored. What did He receive?

Relationship. Honor restored our relationship with our Father. He gets us back when we reciprocate His honor. Even knowing that many would reject His Son, God sent Jesus to die on the cross and assume the sins of the entire world.

The amazing synergy that comes when we reciprocate honor is salvation. Now, stop a moment to think about your relationship with your spouse and how incredibly powerful the synergy can be when both spouses honor and respect in unity. It creates momentum and provides God an incredible vehicle to pour out inheritance upon our families.

Everything pertains to relationships—they're incredibly important to God. Our relationship with God was restored with honor, and honor is the system God has built for blessing our relationships with Him and others. Picture the power of reciprocating honor and receiving salvation, and now imagine the power of honor within your marriage. We don't release this power by keeping rules; we release this power when we honor with grace.

Do you want to see your marriage blessed? Pour honor into it. Do you want to see your marriage explode with inheritance and blessings? Honor and celebrate each other—and get ready for the incredible momentum God will build in your relationship with Him and with one another!

CHAPTER 6

CELEBRATING GOD IN OTHERS

H onor celebrates who someone is rather than who someone *is not*.[2] You might wonder what I mean by that, so let me explain. All too often, we focus on people's weaknesses, the things we don't like, or their mistakes. Instead of looking at personality, style, or anything else that is external, true honor celebrates people for who they are—in Christ.

The funny thing is, when we honor people despite their shortcomings, we create an environment that celebrates what God has placed in their lives. This in turn releases the gifts they carry. If we want to release the gifts within others, if we want to pull inheritance out of others, we honor them and celebrate God in them.

---

2   Bill Johnson and Eric Johnson, *Momentum: What God Starts, Never Ends* (Shippensburg, PA: Destiny Image Pub., 2011), 73.

The Bible is full of examples of people whose gifts were released in an atmosphere of honor. We considered how Jesus honored Peter and drew from him the ministry that birthed the church. Now let's look at another person who honored God and saw increase, Elisha the prophet.

Elisha followed Elijah around for years, learning all the older prophet could teach him. At the end of Elijah's life, Elisha determinedly followed his mentor during the last steps of his life. He had honored this mighty man of God for a long time, and he knew he wanted what the older man possessed.

Let's look at the exchange between the two men right after they crossed the Jordan River in a repeat of God parting the Red Sea: "When they had crossed, Elijah said to Elisha, 'Tell me, what can I do for you before I am taken from you?' 'Let me inherit a double portion of your spirit,' Elisha replied. 'You have asked a difficult thing,' Elijah said, 'yet if you see me when I am taken from you, it will be yours—otherwise, it will not'" (2 Kings 2:9–10).

Elisha had honored what Elijah carried, and the flow of honor between student and teacher pulled the gift out of Elisha. He didn't follow Elijah to receive a double portion, but he understood the principle of inheritance. His motive was not to receive, but he knew that honor would release something valuable.

Elisha, of course, did indeed see Elijah go up to heaven—the famous chariot of fire came by and picked him up for a ride to heaven. Elisha went on to do greater and more numerous miracles than Elijah had done. Honor had drawn out Elisha's gifts.

Honor Values the Seen and Unseen

Our culture places a lot of value on external things like appearance and style. Too often we value what's on the surface and is easily seen, but appearance, as the saying goes, is only skin deep. It can be easy to see the externals and to honor those, but it's something else entirely to honor what is unseen and unappreciated. As a pastor, I've seen people honor me but not the parking lot attendant who helped them find a parking place or the usher who helped them find a seat.

We can do this with our bodies. We pay attention to our faces, our physiques, or even our clothes, but how often do we neglect what's under the skin? We get face-lifts and tummy tucks and do pull-ups, but do we honor the heart that pumps the blood to them and the brain that makes our bodies move? We can see the external, but we can't see what's underneath—yet what's underneath is sometimes the most important of all.

It's easy to see other people's weaknesses and mistakes, style and appearance; it's something else entirely to honor the unseen of who they are in Christ and the gifts He has given them.

Did you know that you can look okay on the outside and yet be sick, even malnourished, on the inside? No one may know that you're not okay on the inside, that what's inside desperately needs to be fixed. If we don't address the needs on the inside, it affects our whole lives.

Nothing on the outside may show that you need help with the pain you feel inside. But if we don't fix what's on the inside, it impacts everything else. We won't function like we should. If we honor only the outside and what is seen, we can miss the things that are inside and unseen but are vitally important. If we honor only the external in ourselves or others but don't look after the internals, our bodies won't function like they should—nor will the body of Christ.

> IF WE HONOR ONLY THE EXTERNAL IN OURSELVES OR OTHERS BUT DON'T LOOK AFTER THE INTERNALS, OUR BODIES WON'T FUNCTION LIKE THEY SHOULD—NOR WILL THE BODY OF CHRIST.

The unseen is real—more real sometimes than what is seen.

This is absolutely true of the things of God. We can see God's workmanship, but He is unseen. Like the wind that moves the limbs of a tree, the Holy Spirit is unseen, yet we see the evidence of His power. The unseen can leave a mark on our seen world, and in fact everything we see actually came from what was unseen.

We can honor the miracles we see from God—healings, breakthroughs, and the like—but if we don't honor the unseen God behind those things and the unseen gifts within the people He works through, I believe we won't see those miracles. Honoring the unseen in the Spirit permits movements of God to be seen. We must honor the seen and unseen, both in the lives of others and in our own lives.

Seeing God in Others and Ourselves

We have amazing opportunities to see good in people and to see God in people—we can see their (perhaps yet unseen) God-given gifts and talents, and we can help them access those through honor. When we don't honor others, it restricts what God is able to do through their lives, just as Jesus was restricted from doing mighty miracles in His hometown. All the hometown folks saw was His flesh; they didn't see the gifts of God. And because of their lack of honor, they didn't experience the benefits of those gifts.

People who came to Jesus in need of a miracle didn't necessarily know He was God. They just knew God was in Jesus. God is in each believer, and when we celebrate God in others, we recognize that He dwells in each of us whether He is seen or not. We also celebrate the gifts He's given to us. After all, who are we *not* to celebrate and honor a gift God has placed in someone? Who are we to dishonor like that?

But here is the tricky part: If you don't honor the gift God has placed in your life, you can hinder it as well. When we see God's gifts within ourselves and honor that, we release God to pour out inheritance on our lives.

People used to prophesy over me when I was growing up. They'd say that God was going to do this or that in my life. But then a voice in my mind would say, "You're not good enough." It was the enemy, and those thoughts sabotaged the gifts in my life because I listened to that voice and didn't honor the gifts.

Sometimes, it's easier to believe in miracles for other people than for ourselves. We can be our own worst critics, dishonoring the gifts God has placed in our lives. God doesn't look at us and judge us. He looks at us through His Son, not through our mistakes. He looks at the God in us, and He honors us and the gifts He's given us. We must do the same.

I've shared that I was horribly insecure as a kid, even though God had spoken to me many times through prophecy. My mom had told me that when I was fifteen, God was going to speak to me—and when she spoke, I listened.

My mom had an incredible connection with the Lord. One time she had a word of knowledge from the Lord that I was at a movie where I shouldn't have been. I was watching a horror movie, and God told her what cinema I was in and which showing. So I was there in the theater when I heard her voice speaking through the darkness, "Is Russell Evans here?" She came in there and pulled me out! So when my mom shared something from the Lord, I listened.

When I was fifteen, a visiting preacher came and spoke at our church. I was on the first row, and a cute girl was behind me. I was "worshipping" God—while eyeing her to see if she noticed how "spiritual" I was—when the speaker suddenly said, "Russell, stand up."

He had disciplined me once when I was younger, so I feared he was going to say I had been worshipping the creation instead of the Creator or something like that. Instead, he said, "Don't compare yourself to your father and mother, your grandfather or your uncle. God has anointed your lips; don't say you're a young man. God will take you to places that will have influence in the world that you wouldn't even dream of. And He's going to anoint your lips with fire, and God's going to be your spokesman."

The problem was, my receptor was wrong, and instead of receiving encouragement from his words, I felt pressured. *After all*, I thought, *I can't communicate. How can I do that?* So instead of receiving and honoring what he said, I listened to a voice that said, "You can't do this,"—even though God had just said I could.

A few years later, another prophet was scheduled to speak at our young adult camp, where I was supposed to play guitar. I had secretly decided I wasn't going to go to the camp. I didn't want to hear another prophecy that would only leave me feeling insecure.

So I decided not to go, but my youth pastor, the emotional Italian, called and asked if I was coming. "Oh, yeah," I lied.

"Well," he said, "I was just in prayer, and God showed me you didn't want to come because you don't want to hear another prophecy."

I was a little upset. *"God, would You please stop telling other people my stuff? Can't we just have some secrets?"*

"Would you please come?" he asked. I was softhearted, so I told him I'd come. Later I prayed, *"All right, God, here's Your opportunity."*

So the day of the event, I stood in line while this man prophesied over people. Basically, I pretended to be spiritual, while in reality I watched what he was doing down the line of people waiting to be prayed for. I watched him through squinted eyes—looking very holy with my hands raised. But when he came in front of me, he paused . . . and then walked on. He didn't say one word to me, although he had shared prophecies for everyone else—just not me.

"That's it, God, I'm finished," I said later. "I gave You an opportunity to speak to me, and that's it—I just can't live with this uncertainty."

Right then my youth pastor poked his head into the building and came up to me. "Let's take a walk," he suggested. We walked for a time, and then he said, "Don't give up on God, Russell." I hadn't said a thing to him. Then, he started crying—and I'm really a sucker for tears. "Don't give up on God," he pleaded through his tears.

> RIGHT THEN I FELT GOD SPEAK VERY QUIETLY INTO MY SPIRIT, "JUST WANT ME."

I replied, "Okay," perhaps just to get away. But later a friend of mine found me and told me some things that God had showed him for me. On the outside, I smiled at him, but inside I dishonored what God had showed him. "You're no prophet," I thought, "you're just my friend."

Right then I felt God speak very quietly into my spirit, "Just want Me."

The next day I went to the meeting and didn't pay much attention to what the speaker said. I went to the altar and crumpled there. "Jesus, I love You," I prayed. "I just love You."

I felt a ray of warmth and love. "I love you, too," God told me. For the next half hour, I experienced God's incredible love and warmth.

The prophet who spoke that day interrupted my conversation with God and said to me, "If you want to be an evangelist, God will release evangelism into your life."

That was *exactly* what my friend had said the night before. "If you want to pastor, God has that gift for you. This is what He says to you—whatever you want to do, He will give it to you." The prophet repeated almost the identical words my friend had spoken the previous night.

All I could say was, "Jesus, I love You," and God replied right back. *"I love you, too. And I want to use you."*

Useful to God

People don't want to be used; we don't like the sound of that. But if you want to be of any use, you must be useful to God. You must admit that you have a use. That use involves the gifts God has placed inside you, and when you honor them, you draw them out.

God told me during that meeting, *"I want to use you,"* but I had an immediate insecurity that sprang up. "I can't communicate," I told Him.

"Yes you can," He answered. *"Here is My power."*

I later looked up that word *power* and I found one of the main Scriptures of my life: Acts 1:8. It says, "But you will receive power when the Holy Spirit comes on you; and you will be my witnesses in Jerusalem, and in all Judea and Samaria, and to the ends of the earth." *Power* here means ability, efficiency, and might.

So God said He would give me *His* ability, efficiency, and might—not for myself, but for others. Out of the

> IF YOU WANT TO BE OF ANY USE, YOU MUST BE USEFUL TO GOD.

empowerment of God's Spirit in your life, He releases you to be who you're called to be—not for yourself, but to influence the world around you.

That night, I finally decided to honor what God had said over me.

Now, I didn't become an amazing communicator overnight. I had to work on my communication skills, but I made the decision to replace the insecurity that had been sabotaging God's gift in my life with honor. If I had continued to believe the lie that I couldn't communicate, I would have hindered God's ability to move in my life. I had to let go of the devil's lie and accept God's power. In my own weakness, I wasn't able to do all that God had spoken over my life, but with His power, I could. I finally came into agreement with what He had said, and I honored it.

From that day forward, I lived with the belief that God's power in me *could*. I became a small-group leader. They gave me thirty young people to look after . . . and I lost twenty of them the first week! But I kept honoring God's words to me. Within two months the group grew to fifty, so we partitioned it—broke into two groups. It grew to another fifty, and eventually they said I could take over the teen youth ministry. It had twenty kids in it, but God grew it to three hundred in less than two years. Eventually, God expanded it to a thousand kids.

If God can use an insecure pastor's kid, He can use anyone. If you will honor what He says about you, it will be released through you. The key to unlocking your gifts and the gifts of those around you is to see God in them—then draw it out through honor. Honor and celebrate the people around you and the gifts God has placed within them, but honor the gifts He has placed in you, too.

When you do, you unlock His power to do great things through your life.

CHAPTER 7

A VALUE OF THE HEART

Have you ever thought that life has a lot of "chicken bones" in it? The thing is, when I eat a piece of chicken, I don't stop eating just because there are some bones in it. I take the bones out, and I put them on the side of my plate.

A lot of Christians cease to honor or turn to lip service when they find "bones" in a ministry or in a person. Instead of enjoying the goodness and celebrating what is rich and meaningful, they want nothing to do with it. We don't do that with good food, but we do that in our lives and with honor. We stop giving honor, or we resort to lip service.

When I was in Bible college, I was a good musician. So everyone told me, "You're going to be a great music director." Yet I felt led to preach, not to be a music director.

Well, one time I was playing guitar for a pastor's conference and under the Spirit of God I played a solo. The presence of God was strong. After the worship, I was really hungry, so I thought I'd sneak out and grab a burger while the speaker preached. I planned to be back in time for the altar call.

I had just gotten into my car when someone ran up and knocked on my window. The speaker, whom I'd never met before, was asking for me! Now, I wasn't leaving to be disrespectful; I was just hungry. So I got out of my car and headed back into the service.

When I came in, the speaker said, "God has just shown me that the next great music out of this nation is coming from you! There's Hillsong, and then you're going to be another sound that comes out of this nation."

Now, my interpretation of what he said was this: you're going to be a music director. But I didn't want to be a music director. So I faced a decision about whether I would honor this word of God or not. Would I choke on the "bones," or would I focus on the good?

I decided I would honor that word from God.

Years later when God called me to start Planetshakers, I felt like He was telling me to take the "bones" out and just put the "chicken" on show. I honored that word to me, and God has honored Planetshakers. We have a conference with amazing speakers, but we're not known for our speakers—we're known for our music. It's the second most widely recognized music to come out of Australia after Hillsong. Instead of rejecting that word or giving lip service to it, I had to say, *"All right, God, I don't understand this, but I honor You."*

Honor Is a Value of the Heart

Honor that doesn't come from the heart isn't really honor at all. The Lord told the prophet Isaiah, "These people come near to me with their mouth and honor me with their lips, but their hearts are far from me. Their worship of me is based on merely human rules they have been taught" (Isaiah 29:13). And He wasn't just speaking of the Israelites.

This is a big deal. I hear people who know the right words to say, but their actions don't line up with their words. True honor is a heart issue not just a word issue. It isn't enough to know the language—we show what we believe by what we *do*, for we act based on the beliefs we hold in our hearts.

Judas is a great example of someone who knew all the right words to say, who could put on a religious mask and masquerade with the best of them. But we know that despite being with Jesus for three years, he had a terminal heart problem. He saw all the miracles; he heard all the sermons. But he didn't honor those opportunities and embrace the heart change that transforms from the inside out.

HONOR THAT DOESN'T COME FROM THE HEART ISN'T REALLY HONOR AT ALL.

We interpret everything through our hearts—through our beliefs. Our hearts are the filters for everything—not our minds. If you doubt this, just consider whether you have ever let your feelings and beliefs color the facts. I see it all the time in our meetings. One person will worship Jesus and really receive from the Lord, and right next to her is someone who doesn't honor the music or the teaching. He stands with his arms crossed, a frown on his face. It's the same message, same song—but different hearts. One honors in her heart, the other doesn't.

Guess which one receives from the Lord?

Soft Heart, Strong Mind

You see, God doesn't want you to have a hard heart and a soft head; God wants you to have a soft heart and a strong mind. What happens is that we can harden our hearts—but then our thinking gets soft. It takes a lot more strength of mind to keep a soft heart than it does to have a hard heart. It's easy to have a hard heart.

If we keep a soft heart in all things, we are movable and pliable to the Lord. He can move our hearts, impress things upon us, and guide us. A soft heart is better in relationships. Many guys think they need to be strong, shouldn't ever cry, and need to be hard. Women understand better: they would rather have a man with a heart that can be moved than a rock-hard rock star who can't be moved by anything.

GOD WANTS YOU TO HAVE A SOFT HEART AND A STRONG MIND.

From the day we got married, my wife and I decided we wouldn't go on to the next day with an issue or argument between us—we wouldn't go to bed until we'd worked it through. We knew we had to deal with heart issues right away, because if we waited, we knew we'd start moving toward hard hearts. You want a soft heart toward your spouse, but you need a soft heart in your relationship with God even more.

Rather than a hard heart, we need to have a strong mind. A strong mind pulls down and demolishes "arguments and every pretension that sets itself up against the knowledge of God, and we take captive every thought to make it obedient to Christ" (2 Corinthians 10:5). A strong mind isn't vulnerable to the lies and fears of the enemy; it's full of power and love (2 Timothy 1:7).

A soft heart will give honor without expecting a return. It will look for the unseen and will draw the gifts out of others. With soft hearts we submit our gifts to the Lord. A soft heart is the kind of heart God can work with.

Determining the Real You

So what do you do if you know you're hard-hearted? The slow process of time has burned you and made you jaded. You've had promises go unfulfilled, been disappointed, hurt, and abandoned. Maybe you feel God is the guilty party to these hurts and honoring anything from Him seems difficult, if not impossible.

The Jews had reason to feel the same way. Their hard hearts eventually led to exile, but God offered a great promise to all who would turn around and head home: "I will give them an undivided heart and put a new spirit in them; I will remove from them their heart of stone and give them a heart of flesh" (Ezekiel 11:19).

This transformation from the inside out is the result of honor.

The above promise is good, you might think, but what are some practical steps toward that kind of transformation? For that, I would like to come back to our words. A moment ago I shared that words alone are not enough. You can't just give lip service to God and expect to receive an inheritance. But—and this is important—words are *a start.*

Your words form your world. Part of the process to change your heart is to change your speech, and some of us need to stop listening to ourselves and start *talking* to ourselves. Remember that little voice that would tell me I couldn't communicate? I had to stop listening to it. I had to start declaring prophetically over my life that what *God* had said was true, and I did it out loud.

A favorite prophetic passage of the Bible says, "Let the weak say, 'I am strong' " (Joel 3:10). God told the people to declare what was not yet true as though it were true. In our modern context, we might say "But that's not being authentic, that's not being real"—which is correct. It isn't real. It's not natural. It's *super*natural.

Earlier, I asked you, "Which *you* are you? The flesh *you,* or the spirit *you?*" At our church and in our conferences, we encounter people who don't want to raise their hands or express themselves passionately in worship. They say, "Well, that just isn't *me.*" Some even say they *want* to express themselves, but they don't think they're being real and authentic when they raise their hands. That's when I ask them which is real—the flesh or the spirit—and I remind them which one is going to live eternally.

Saying something prophetically over your life is kingdom-thinking, and it comes from the spirit-you—the real you. It's real in the kingdom of God, for if God said it as though it were true, *it is*. We just may not see it yet.

It's good to honor with your words, but the real power comes when your heart backs up your words. It seems paradoxical, but you can change your heart by getting your words in order. However, lasting heart change comes from the inside out. Your words are only the beginning of the transformation process, but that's a good place to start.

More on the Unseen

We don't understand everything that happens in our lives, but we can still speak out prophetically over our lives and honor what God is doing. Sometimes that requires looking intently for the unseen in our lives and the lives of others to find what God wants us to honor.

Joyce Meyer, who came from an abusive background, shared that at one point God asked her why she wasn't honoring her father. When she complained that she couldn't honor abuse, the Lord confirmed that, indeed, she shouldn't honor the abuse, but she *could* honor the fact that her father had clothed and fed her.

Sometimes, to find something to honor we must look intently for the unseen. And in circumstances like hers, you can understand how important a soft heart was—it allowed her to forgive and then to honor her father, regardless of how he responded.

In case you're worried that a soft heart will leave you vulnerable, let me assure you that it will—vulnerable to God. That's why we need to have strong minds, and we need to exercise discernment and wisdom, because how we honor is dictated by wisdom.

I mentioned that getting a hard heart is easy, but we want to know how to keep a soft one. Let's look at two ways the Lord has made real to me.

Keep the Dove in Mind

God enables us to keep a soft heart through the power of His Spirit. When you worship God and love on Jesus, you don't think about your enemies. Your heart is submitted to the Lord and you think about Him. If you do think of those who have hurt you, your attitude toward them is probably soft because your heart is tender toward God. So how do we bring that same experience into everyday life?

We must understand who we are in Christ. We must be conscious of His presence with us. How? We must walk with the Dove in mind.

When John baptized Jesus in the Jordan, the Bible tells us that the Holy Spirit alighted on Him like a dove (John 1:32). Jesus' earthly ministry began after that, for He was filled with power.

A SOFT HEART LETS JESUS CONSUME OUR HURT WITH HIS LOVE.

If you had the Holy Spirit Dove perched on your shoulder, wouldn't you live differently? You would move with care, because you wouldn't want Him to fly off. You would walk with the Dove in mind, and you wouldn't do anything that would make Him fly away.[3]

In the same way, if you want a soft heart you must live with the Dove in mind. You must walk conscious of God's presence in your life, because He's not perched on your shoulder, He's in your heart.

Life constantly presents opportunities to let our hearts crust over, but if the Resident of our hearts were tangible, sitting on our shoulders, would we live and react differently? What would you do when your spouse or another person hurt your feelings if Jesus were visible to you? If Jesus were in a room together with you and an enemy, what would consume your thoughts—Jesus, or your unforgiveness or hate? A soft heart lets Jesus consume our hurt with His love.

We must walk with the Dove in mind.

Praise God

Another key to a soft heart is thanksgiving. It's impossible to be depressed or hurt and thankful at the same time. In God's presence, perhaps during worship, we move our thinking from ourselves to Him. This is easy to do when the music is playing and the atmosphere is one of worship, but we can make a conscious decision to maintain an attitude of thanksgiving when we are not worshipping, just like we can decide to walk at

---

3   Bill Johnson, *Hosting the Presence: Unveiling Heaven's Agenda* (Shippensburg, PA: Destiny Image Pub., 2012), 115.

all times with the Dove in mind. We can choose to be thankful and to praise God regardless of our circumstances.

What if you don't feel like you have anything to be thankful for?

Well, there are times when everything seems down and life is discouraging, but we can universally, always, perpetually praise and thank God, because He is good. I have a problem with people who say God causes sickness or God uses sickness to teach us something. As a dad, if I ever used sickness to teach my children a lesson, I'd be jailed as a child abuser.[4] God is not a child abuser; in fact, He is the opposite.

Now, do we learn through difficult experiences? Yes. But God is not the author of those experiences. He doesn't create the problem. Sin creates the problem—a fallen world creates the problem.

The Bible tells us to "give thanks in all circumstances" (1 Thessalonians 5:18). Notice it doesn't say *for* all circumstances but *in* all circumstances. It also declares that "we know that in all things God works for the good of those who love him, who have been called according to his purpose" (Romans 8:28).

He wants us to come before Him with thanksgiving and praise—not just at church, but all the time. Anytime. He wants us to walk with the Dove in mind and to be thankful in all circumstances. It's God's modus operandi. He doesn't need our praises and thanksgiving, but He wants us to experience Him through our praise and thanksgiving. He wants to pour out inheritance upon us. He wants us to experience heaven.

---

4   Bill Johnson, *When Heaven Invades Earth: A Practical Guide to a Life of Miracles* (Shippensburg, PA: Destiny Image Pub., 2005), 21.

My mother understood the power of praise. When I was little and we were missionaries in Papua, New Guinea, she became extremely sick with hepatitis. One morning, she woke up to see a massive snake hanging above her, and something snapped in her mind. My dad took a chair and killed the snake, but in her weakened state, her nervous system couldn't handle the shock.

I think she had a nervous breakdown. My father had just accepted a pastoral position, and they had two young boys to care for. Sadly, despite all the doctors, medication, and prayer, she began to smother under a blanket of depression and we had to leave the mission field.

Now, you need to understand that my mother was a strong woman. She wasn't fragile, easily cowed, or quick to self-pity. But the depression was serious, nearly crippling.

As I mentioned earlier, her heart was finely tuned to hear clearly from the Lord. One day she felt Him tell her, *"Praise Me."* "What do You mean, 'Praise Me'"? she asked. "Praise You for *this?"* She heard God reply, *"Praise Me in all things."*

So she made a choice. She honored that word, and every morning, she got up and raised praises to the Lord. "God," she prayed, "You are good. I don't understand what's going on in my life, but I praise you." She worshiped, she praised. She always said that the first few minutes were the most difficult. But as she persisted to praise for five or ten minutes, the heaviness lifted—God promises to exchange our despair for a garment of praise (Isaiah 61:3)—and she walked free for the rest of the day.

One day Jim Spillman, an American evangelist, came to speak in Australia, and at his service my mom went down under the power of the Holy Spirit—with two thousand other people! When she came up, she said she felt like she was drunk. She stayed that way, lost in God's presence, for three days! When she went with my dad to see Spillman off at the airport, he said, "During the meeting, God did something for a woman who had a problem with a snake."

"It was me," my mom told him. My mother passed from this life to a better one a few years ago, but for the rest of her life on earth (and maybe beyond), she helped people who experienced depression or heaviness in their lives. She taught them not to try to understand the circumstances but to praise. She taught them to give thanks in all things and to keep their hearts soft. She taught that we are training to rein in heaven.

The deepest praises come from the softest hearts. It's not about the words we speak, for praises can rise to God even without spoken words. No, it's not just about our words—it's about our hearts.

What have you given your heart to? Money? Appearances? Diversions? If it's anything other than God—even good works—it shows that you value that more than you value the Lord. Do you want to know where your heart is? Consider where you spend your money and your time.

Some people think they simply need to set priorities—put God first and then line up their families, careers, church, hobbies, and so forth to follow. But that's not it at all. We don't put God first and partition up the rest of our lives without Him. He must be first in our lives and in our families and in our careers. He must be first in *everything*. He's the center, and everything else moves around Him.

If He's not at the center of your life, it's not too late to change your heart. It's not too late to receive a heart of tenderness to replace a heart of stone. Start speaking God's words to yourself, live with His presence in mind, and let the fruit of your lips be praise. These things are a good start, but never forget that it's not all about your words. Honor, after all, is a value of the heart.

CHAPTER 8

WOW!—NOT WHY

True honor exists when we embrace two opposing concepts. First, when we honor, we open our lives to receive. Second, true honor doesn't look for anything in return and doesn't give to get. It's an issue of the heart—of motivations. This is the paradox of honor.

We've also talked about honor being about *us,* in the plural, not about *me* in the singular. When honor becomes self-seeking, it misses the point. It misses the heart of God.

This is clearly illustrated by the elder brother in the parable of the prodigal. You'll remember that when the elder brother got near home, he heard a party going on and found out it was because his little brother had returned. Instead of sharing the father's heart of gladness that the prodigal had returned, the elder brother grew angry and refused to come inside.

When the younger brother left with his inheritance, the older brother saw his father's tears and pain and loss. But when the family was restored, the older brother didn't rejoice; he became angry and jealous as the father heaped honor on the younger son.

"You never threw a 'fatted calf' party for me," he complained. "All these years I've slaved, working my fingers to the bone for you, and for what?" The prodigal son's return revealed the true condition of the elder brother's heart and his selfish agenda. His focus was on the reward he felt he deserved. Instead of sharing the father's heart of grace, he selfishly obsessed about what he had earned. He wanted something in return.

When God blesses others, no matter how little we may think they "deserve" it, a person with a true kingdom heart rejoices. They are part of the body of Christ, so their blessing is our blessing. We're all connected!

Besides, what the elder brother didn't recognize was that though the prodigal got the fatted calf, *he owned the farm!* "Everything I have is yours," the father told him (Luke 15:31). But his selfishness caused him to lose his objectivity.

A Bank Check

A friend of mine who was on staff with us was also a school chaplain. He had to interact with a man who was a chaplain somewhere else, and this guy always went against him. He said negative things about my friend, who didn't know what to do about it.

He asked me what I thought he should do, and I said, "Let's wait to see God's hand. Don't be too worried about him." Well, out of the blue God spoke to my friend and told him to send this man a bank check—like a money order. It was to be anonymous, so the man wouldn't know who had sent it.

And God told my friend to make it for a couple *thousand* dollars.

My staff member obeyed. He just wrote "God loves you" on it and sent it. About three months later, my friend ran into this guy and asked how he was doing—now, bear in mind, this man still had an issue with my friend.

"I would've given up on God [because of people like you], but God showed me how much He loved me by sending me two thousand dollars," the man said.

Now, right there my friend had a chance to say, "Hey, *I* sent that!" or simply rejoice with him and say, "Wow, how awesome!" God kept him on track, and he didn't say a thing. He went his way rejoicing that God had showed this man how much He loved him. My friend didn't look for anything in return, even though this man *still had an attitude problem* with him and telling him who had sent the check might have seemed like a way to fix the situation.

> TRUE HONOR DOESN'T LOOK FOR ANYTHING IN RETURN.

But my friend knew that true honor doesn't look for anything in return.

When you step out and decide to live a life of honor, you'll experience these kinds of situations. Someone less deserving will get something you should have received, or something bad will happen to you while something good happens to someone else. You'll face a situation similar to the one my friend faced— you'll have to decide whether you are honoring to get something in return or because you have the heart of your Father.

You'll face situations where people who manipulate, intimidate, and control seem to get ahead. You'll face heart questions about this. But don't be deceived; this type of gain is temporary, and an entitlement mentality toward God will leave your heart out in the cold to harden.

Isaac and Ishmael

It's hard to watch others benefit from the honor you've sown, and it's hard to watch people who scratch and scramble and claw to get ahead. You could say the world's system works—if you're looking for Ishmael.

If you're familiar with the story of Abraham, you know that God promised he would have more descendants than anyone could count and would be the father of many nations. What we often forget is that it didn't take a day, a week, or a month for Abraham to receive his promise—*it took years and years!* While they waited for the promise to come to pass, Abraham and Sarah, his wife, became frustrated and impatient. If you or close friends have tried to conceive and failed, you understand how even the wonder of marital intimacy can become frustrating and pressured. Before you make love, you wonder if you can handle the disappointment again and have *that* hanging over your marriage bed. Now, the Bible tells us that Abraham's faith didn't fail, but he *did* eventually give in to the pressure to try something other than honor. Sarah gave her servant to him, he slept with her, and the result of that attempt to control and manipulate God's promise, was a son—Ishmael.

Abraham didn't abandon honor and stop sleeping with Sarah, and they eventually had Isaac, the child of promise. But the descendants of Ishmael and the descendants of Isaac war with each other *to this day* over the Middle East. How might the entire face of our world be different if Abraham had persevered in honor?

Many people don't understand that our seed is blessed, wherever we sow it. Where you place that seed and what grows from it depends on whether you sow to the kingdom or to the flesh. Ishmael represents the works of the flesh, and Isaac represents the works of the Spirit. Both seeds are blessed, because in its DNA it's blessed, and this is why manipulation, intimidation, and

> *WHEN YOU LIVE GOD'S WAY AND SOW YOUR SEED INTO HIS KINGDOM, YOU WON'T REAP A HARVEST OF THE FLESH, YOU'LL REAP A HARVEST OF ETERNAL INHERITANCE.*

control can seem to move things forward as a counterfeit for honor. But even if you experience what the world calls "success" by counterfeiting, you can't truly prosper because your soul isn't prospering. When you live God's way and sow your seed into His kingdom, you won't reap a harvest of the flesh, you'll reap a harvest of eternal inheritance.

Why Ask "Why"?

Where does promotion come from? The Bible tells us that promotion comes from God (Psalm 75:6–7 KJV). So if promotion comes from God, we honor what He has promoted, even though we don't understand it. We covered a similar topic when we said that God appoints people to our lives, but here we see that God is in our circumstances and timing.

It's not an easy subject. In fact, we make arguments against it to back up our opinions. We've made entire doctrines to help God out. People say that God causes sickness or that God doesn't want to heal everybody or that God sends natural disasters to punish people. Why? Because when life disappoints, we look for a way to wrap our minds around the situation and understand—rather than wrap our soft hearts around God and trust.

My mother died of cancer, and I can choose two ways of responding to that. I can cope by saying that God gives and God takes away and fixate on why it happened. Or, I can have His heart and praise Him through every circumstance, saying, "God, you're good. I press into you. I don't understand everything, but that's not my job. My job is to believe, it's not to make excuses for why certain things happen or don't happen."

When I stand before God in heaven, the first thing out of my mouth won't be "Why?" The first thing out of my mouth will be "Wow!" It will be praise, and I want the things that come out of my mouth here on earth to be the same as they will be there.

A transformed mind doesn't need to ask why. It is like His mind, and it matches a heart soft to Him here on earth—a heart

He can move and influence now, not just when we go to heaven. His ways are higher than our ways, and His thoughts are higher than our thoughts (Isaiah 55:9), but He wants us to have His ways and His thoughts. We do this through a transformed mind.

Intimacy

A few pages ago, I spoke of intimacy in the terms of a husband and wife who want to receive a promise. Just as a husband and wife come together to see their seed blessed and result in a promise, so, too, intimacy with God births the promises in our lives.

When you're close to God, you have the right perspective. In His presence, you think of things differently. When you're intimate with Him, you are productive—you experience fruit by exchanging your perspective for His, your cold heart of stone for one of flesh.

From the beginning of life here on earth, God commanded that "like would reproduce like." It's a fundamental truth—dogs come together to produce dogs, birds produce birds, and people produce people. What you are intimate with is what you will produce.

When the real you, the spirit you, comes together in honor with the Spirit of God, you produce the fruit of blessings and inheritance. When you're intimate with your problems, or things like bitterness or a mentality of entitlement, you produce that kind of fruit.

WHAT YOU HONOR IS WHAT YOU BECOME.

What you honor is what you become.

So what kind of fruit do you want to produce? The fruit of selfishness, like the elder brother, or the fruit of grace and inheritance, like the prodigal? Who correctly understood the heart of the father—the elder son, who wouldn't come into the celebration, or the prodigal, who received his father's honor? I would argue that after all was said and done, the prodigal understood his father and shared his heart.

We choose what we honor, and what we honor determines what we become.

CHAPTER 9

START WALKING

I n a previous chapter I mentioned that while Jesus was here on earth people may not have known He was God, but they could see God in Him. This same concept is at the center of honoring and celebrating others for the presence of God in their lives and for the gifts He has given them. The paradox is that when we honor, this releases inheritance—yet we don't expect to receive anything back.

We practice honor by thinking of others and not ourselves, and we accept that anything we receive in return is merely a fringe benefit. Only then can we move into a deeper understanding of how God uses honor as a vehicle to bless us. Without the groundwork of the previous chapters, which focused on our hearts and our motives, we won't understand why we honor and how we handle what we receive because of honor.

Bottom line: We've got to keep our eyes on Jesus and the body of Christ—not on ourselves.

In the book of John, we find one of the best stories about someone who saw God in Jesus—it's the story of how Jesus healed a nobleman's son. As Jesus was traveling through Galilee, He passed through Cana, where He had turned water into wine. A nobleman from nearby Capernaum heard that Jesus was in the region, so he went to Him and begged Him to heal his son, who was close to death.

Jesus' response is a bit surprising: "'Unless you people see signs and wonders,' Jesus told him, 'you will never believe'" (John 4:48). But the nobleman wasn't dissuaded, and he implored Jesus to come to his house before his son died.

This is where the story gets interesting: "Jesus said to him, 'Go your way; your son lives.' So the man believed the word that Jesus spoke to him, and he went his way" (John 4:50 NKJV).

Now, this nobleman would be a person of note, of royalty perhaps; one translation calls him a government official. This man understood honor, and he had the power and authority to make people do what he said. But he came and implored Jesus, calling Him (who appeared to be merely a carpenter's son) "Sir" or "Lord."

Despite Jesus' apparent frustration with the Jews—I think I can hear some irritation as He wondered aloud if the Jews would ever believe without miraculous signs—He gave the man a word, a command. "Go back home, your son will live."

The man had no assurance that Jesus would do as He promised—just a word. We have the luxury of reading the next verse to find out what happened, but this man didn't have that.

The Bible tells us that he believed the word Jesus spoke and he turned to go home.

He started walking.

As he neared his home, his servants ran to him and told him the good news that his son was alive—he had been healed. The nobleman asked when it had happened, and the servants told him what time it was: the same time Jesus had given him the word that his son would live. Because of this, the nobleman and his whole household believed in God.

> *PRAYER IS NOT BEGGING GOD SO MUCH AS HUMBLING OURSELVES BEFORE HIM.*

Note that before his family received the inheritance of salvation—before he knew his son was healed—he had to start walking.

Humble

This powerful story is a compelling example of honor. Jesus was in Cana and not in his hometown because He had found no honor there. He knew that the effectiveness of His life wasn't determined by His gifts but how His gifts were honored. And we know that where the people honored His gifts and the power of God in His life, He did great miracles. Where they did not, He could do little.

This nobleman honored Jesus. Despite his status in society, the Bible says that he *begged* Jesus to heal his son. That word *beg* in the original language implies the sense of "humbling oneself," so this man humbled himself before Jesus and honored Him.

This is a terrific representation of prayer. Prayer is not begging God so much as humbling ourselves before Him. We see this illustrated in another story, that of the Pharisee and the tax collector. The Pharisee praised himself in his prayer, while the tax collector humbly repented. "I tell you that this man, rather than [the Pharisee], went home justified before God. For all those who exalt themselves will be humbled, and those who humble themselves will be exalted," Jesus tells us (Luke 18:14).

A Christian who stops praying is a Christian who thinks he is God. He has made himself the god of his life, and he feels no need to honor God by humbling himself in prayer.

Due to his position, the nobleman had the authority to give orders to a carpenter. But he didn't. He humbled himself because He saw God in Jesus—and this was before Jesus had raised Lazarus and done a host of other miracles. Not only that, but the man persisted in his request, even when Jesus gave him an answer that would send people deserting our churches in droves if we gave it from the pulpit today.

The nobleman honored the carpenter, even when it seemed that he was not honored in return and would not receive the inheritance he sought.

Walk Toward the Promise

One of the key points of this story is that we honor what we walk toward. Before this man knew his son was healed, he honored Jesus' word to him and walked towards the promise. He headed home, in obedience to what Jesus had told him to do.

This simple act demonstrated that he honored Jesus' word and that he believed.

Do you think it was easy for him? Consider how long it took for him to experience the inheritance his honor had released. The Bible tells us that the boy was healed at the very moment Jesus instructed the nobleman to head home, around 1:00 in the afternoon. But the nobleman didn't learn that his son was healed until the next day, when he met his servants on his way home. That means he walked all day, through the afternoon, and into the evening. We don't know if he stopped to rest, but his journey took him through the dark of night before he learned his son was healed.

What kept him going through that long walk and through the night? He honored what Jesus had spoken when he started walking. Then he kept walking, kept believing. I believe it was honor that kept him going.

It's easy to believe right after the Lord has spoken. We get all excited when we receive a word or a promise, but sometimes we have to walk all day and through the darkest of nights before we receive the inheritance our honor has released. During that walk, we can feel alone—Jesus was back in Cana, and the nobleman was on his way to Capernaum. We can feel isolated. It seems that God is nowhere to be found.

When you're waiting for God's word to be fulfilled, when it's dark and you feel alone, will you give up? Will you stop in the valley of the shadow of death and make camp?

Or will you keep walking?

The psalmist wrote, "Though I walk *through* the valley of the shadow of death, I will fear no evil" (Psalm 23:4 NKJV, emphasis mine). Why? Because while the valley is mentioned in verse four, the *promise* is given in verse five: "You prepare a table before me in the presence of my enemies; You anoint my head with oil; my cup runs over" (Psalm 23:5 NKJV).

There are only a few paths out of the darkest night: We can turn around and go back; we can wander off course; we can set up camp there in the valley; or we can keep walking toward our promise. We honor what we walk toward.

All too often we think we know what God is going to do. We go to Jesus thinking that He will come with us so we can receive our inheritance. Or we receive a word from Him, but the path toward the promise isn't what we expected—it takes us through the night.

Sometimes God walks us through the night so He can be the lamp unto our feet and the light for our path. Sometimes, He gives us a promise He knows is far too big for us when He gives it. He knows we must walk in faith while He increases our spiritual strength, and when we are ready to receive the promise, we will do so with respect because we have been through the journey of honor.

So will you honor God's words to you? If so, it's time to start walking.

Through Every Season

A heart of honor walks toward God's promises in every season and pursues what God has said to do—even when it doesn't see the fruit in that season.

My grandparents were incredible people whose lives demonstrated faithful honor. Many years ago, in Wales, a preacher stopped his sermon to ask my grandfather, a young coal miner, if he was saved. My grandfather gave his life to Christ in that meeting. Across the world, my grandmother was saved in a Smith Wigglesworth crusade in Australia. As single people they each moved to India to be missionaries. There they met and eventually married.

Here's an amazing thing about their missionary work and where honor comes into the picture: In their first five years of ministry, they had *one* person decide to follow Christ.

> WE HONOR WHAT WE WALK TOWARD.

One. They didn't see much impact for all their faithful efforts, but God's call kept them going. They ministered in India for twenty-five more years, and when they returned to Australia, they left behind many churches and disciples. Just a few years ago, my father went back to India to dedicate a building for a ministry that began under my grandfather's leadership. An elderly lady ran up to him and began to weep over his feet. "Beautiful feet" (Isaiah 52:7) she said over and over as she cried. She was the first person to give her life to Christ under my grandfather's ministry.

My grandparents' faithful honor gave birth to my father's ministry, which added tremendously to the work of God and nurtured my own life and ministry. Planetshakers has had an impact worldwide, but I firmly believe it would have had no impact if my grandparents had not honored God for those first five years in India during a long, dark night.

Walking Takes Steps

True honor follows up words and thoughts with actions. The actions that honor God are as diverse as His callings on our lives, which are all unique, but have some things in common. We can honor Him with our money, and we may give to His cause. We honor Him by praying and interceding for people, groups, even countries. We forgive those who have hurt us, and we care for those who lack resources.

As "faith without works is dead" (James 2:20), so honor without works is dead. Honor and faith are best friends. True honor leads to true action.

One of the clearest Scriptures about a step of honor comes from the wisest man who ever lived. Solomon wrote, "Honor the LORD with your wealth, with the firstfruits of all your crops" (Proverbs 3:9). That's a step in walking. The by-product is that God reciprocates that honor, and we see the inheritance in the next verse: "Then your barns will be filled to overflowing, and your vats will brim over with new wine" (Proverbs 3:10).

TRUE HONOR LEADS TO TRUE ACTION.

This is just one example of a step we can take to honor the Lord and His Word. You see, God doesn't need your money. Your pastor doesn't need your money. God is the source of every good thing, and when we return the tithe to Him and give offerings, we honor Him with our wealth and free Him to pour out inheritance on us.

Nothing will keep you going like seeing God's promises in action and seeing Him pour out inheritance on your life!

Honor What Keeps You Going

The nobleman whose son was healed left Jesus without getting what he came for: Jesus going with him to Capernaum. But he received what he needed—a word from the Lord, a promise. During his long walk home, through the night, what kept him going? What kept him putting one foot in front of the other?

Faith kept him going. Not faith in what Jesus had done, for the man hadn't seen that yet—he had no confirmation. He had to have faith in who Jesus was, and he could have that faith because he saw God in Jesus.

If we honor God only when we feel like it, our honor will waver when our feelings waver. But if we honor what God says, who He is, and what He's called us to do, God Himself will keep us going. Our faith pleases God and allows us to access and depend on His strength and fuel for the journey rather than our own limited supplies.

> *HONOR AND FAITH WILL KEEP YOU GOING, EVEN WHEN THE FACTS SEEM TO CONTRADICT GOD'S WORD TO YOU.*

Currency

Honor and faith will keep you going, even when the facts seem to contradict God's word to you.

When you honor the natural realm, you receive the natural "facts." For example, when you honor a natural medical diagnosis, you receive that condition in your body. The spiritual truth is the opposite—by Christ's stripes you are healed. Honoring this spiritual truth will result in receiving supernatural healing. If you honor the natural human response to being hurt by someone, you'll most likely hurt that person back and the situation will get worse. Instead, if you honor the kingdom principle of forgiveness, you will reap the fruit of forgiveness in your own life. Honoring God, His Word, and His kingdom will release the supernatural fruit of miracles, breakthroughs, and blessings into your life every time!

You can honor "facts" or *truth,* and when you honor the truth of what God says, you release the supernatural in your life. You don't ignore the facts, you just apply God's truth to them!

When we release truth into our situation instead of fact, we release honor and faith into our lives, and these become a medium of exchange. Honor and faith are the currency of heaven.

If I walked into a store and grabbed an iPad and headed for the door without paying, I'd be arrested because I would have taken something that wasn't mine. I have to use currency to make it mine. Sometimes we act like that with God. We ask for something, but we don't believe for it. We don't honor what He says about something, even though we asked about it. We don't have faith for it. Then we get frustrated when we don't get it.

Why don't we receive when we ask? Because we don't believe and honor what God says.

Do you want to see miracles? Do you want to see a breakthrough? Do you want to see heaven come to earth in your life? Receive what He tells you—and start walking.

Press In

Have you ever been so desperate for something that you were willing to do whatever it took to get it? Have you ever craved a breakthrough so much that you were willing to push through every adversity to receive it?

A woman in the Bible did this, and she gives us a terrific example of someone who held onto something and kept walking until she received it. But she didn't just walk—she took it to another level. She pressed in.

This woman had heard of Jesus, and while He was on His way to save a little girl's life, she pressed through the crowd surrounding Him. She had been sick for twelve years, and while she had tried everything to improve her health, she was no better. In fact, all the doctors and all her efforts had only made things *worse*.

She was desperate. So desperate, she went against Jewish law to stand in the crowd with her issue. But she thought, "If I just touch his clothes, I will be healed" (Mark 5:28).

This woman didn't honor the facts. The facts said that the doctors had done all they could and she would never get better. After all, if her health hadn't improved in twelve years, why would it improve now? Yet she didn't think this way—she didn't put weight behind that.

She put weight behind the belief that if she touched the edge of Jesus' robe she would be healed. So she didn't honor the conventions of those pressing around her and threatening to keep her away from Him; she pressed on until she came up behind Him through the throng. She stretched out her hand, straining to touch Him.

She didn't honor the crowd, because the crowd tried to push her out; she honored Jesus, who touched her in the crowd. The very place she shouldn't have been was the place where she received from Jesus.

HER FAITH AND HONOR RELEASED THE POWER OF JESUS INTO HER LIFE.

Her true honor led to true action. This woman pushed in—she believed, and she wouldn't be denied. Though she was broke in earthly currency, having spent all she had trying to get better, her stretched-out hand conveyed that she was rich in the currency of heaven. Weakened by twelve years of loss, she still found the strength to press in through the obstacles and limitations to cash in her faith and honor for the miracle she desperately needed.

Her faith and honor released the power of Jesus into her life.

This woman didn't just honor what she walked toward— she honored what she pressed in for, what she strained toward with all of her strength and determination.

What would you do if you were desperate? How hard would you press in? How urgently would you stretch out in faith and honor if a crowd stood between you and Jesus, between you and the miracle or breakthrough you needed?

Most of us would say that we would do whatever it took, and press through any crowd, if Jesus were standing in the flesh before us.

We think that if Jesus showed up in our home, in our situation, we would believe. We would have faith. The problem is, Jesus showed up in His own town, and they didn't believe. He was there, *right there,* and they received virtually nothing from Him when they could have received *everything.*

The nobleman thought that if Jesus would just come home with him, his son would be healed. But Jesus didn't come home with him—Jesus sent him home with a word—a promise. The nobleman simply had to believe. He had to press on through the day and through the night, and with the dawn he found that his son had been healed.

Sometimes it's not enough to walk. Sometimes you must press in and not let anything deter you from believing the word the Lord has given you. Press on, friend. Don't let go, and don't turn back. Keep on through the dark of night, trusting Him to be the light for your feet. Your breakthrough will come with the dawn if you'll accept God's strength to keep going, to exchange the currency of honor and faith for the inheritance God wants to give you.

CHAPTER 10

HONOR IN MOTION

God is always speaking. Every Sunday, pastors deliver words from the pulpit, and every time we pick up the Bible, God speaks to us through His Word. We can hear His words in our spirits if we listen.

It's our job to determine if what we hear in our spirits lines up with the Word and character of God, but the thing I want to touch on here is our response. People who sit next to each other in church can have wildly different experiences in their lives because one honors the Word and the other doesn't.

Through many years of church life, I've seen people respond in different ways to a word from the Lord. Often God has spoken to me about things He wants to do at that time or in the future. Once He gives the word, the question is, will His people respond?

A word from God might be that He wants to heal people of back conditions. When a man sitting in the front row with a back condition hears that word, he has a choice. He can honor that word, or he can be cynical. He can sit there and wonder whether the word is for him, or he can stand up and say that he accepts the promise for himself.

The difference is honor. He can choose to honor—or not. Your pastor can declare God's word to you, but you must choose to respond.

When Jesus told the nobleman, "Go home, your son is healed," that was the word declared. That man had no reference to turn to in the Bible to confirm Jesus' word; he simply had the testimony that he saw God in Jesus. By acting in honor, he participated in the power that words have to form our worlds.

Now, I'm not saying that you must blindly believe every "word" that comes from anyone who claims to have a word from God. We must test every word from God to ensure it lines up with the Word of God.

WE MUST TEST EVERY WORD FROM GOD TO ENSURE IT LINES UP WITH THE WORD OF GOD.

I want to focus on the corporate setting for a moment. If you're in church and the pastor says he has a particular vision for the church, you have a choice of honor or cynicism. You can say, "Yeah, I've heard stuff like that before"—and that cynical spirit and pessimism will be exactly what you receive from the pastor's word. Or you can say, "Yes and amen," to the word and add your currency of faith and honor to what God wants to do in the church—and in your life.

When you honor the word declared in your life, you put agreement to the work God wishes to do in and around you. Yet true honor isn't just thinking in agreement, it's *acting* in agreement.

What It Takes to Save the World

One year, I received a word from God that He wanted to make it a year of favor for our church. I encouraged the congregation to believe God for new jobs and financial breakthroughs. What did that do? It allowed people to come into agreement for new jobs and breakthroughs. But truly honoring that word didn't mean that people could agree with me then wait for God to do the rest. People had to look for new jobs. People had to believe God to bring financial breakthrough . . . then we received reports of how God backed up their actions with blessings.

The nobleman honored Jesus' word. What did he do? He put his faith into action and headed home. What must we do to receive inheritance from God? We must agree with His declared word and put our faith and honor into action.

Do you remember the story we mentioned at the beginning of this book, when Jesus turned water into wine at the wedding in Cana? It was His first miracle. But did you know that this miracle teaches us how to save the world?

> WHAT MUST WE DO TO RECEIVE INHERITANCE FROM GOD? WE MUST AGREE WITH HIS DECLARED WORD AND PUT OUR FAITH AND HONOR INTO ACTION.

What did the servants have to do when Jesus gave them a word? They had to dip a ladle into a water jar and take it to the master of ceremonies. They had to act. They had to obey.

Do you know that if every Christian did what God has told us to do the world would be saved? Simply acting in honor and faith, in agreement with His word (or Word), is enough to accomplish God's will for the whole earth. Imagine what could happen for God's kingdom if millions of His sons and daughters on the planet acted on every word that comes from His lips. The results would be awesome, unstoppable.

But instead, what happens? We're on the bus and God tells us, "Go tell that person I love them," and what do we do? Our flesh comes up and says, "What will they think?" Or He tells us to give anonymously in order to bless someone, and when we give we shift the spotlight from God to ourselves by telling who gave it.

I've heard so many people use this excuse: "Well, I didn't know it was God." Or, "How do I know if the impression I have is from God?" Well, let me just declare by the power of the Holy Spirit, if it's good, it's from God. Praying for someone is good; it's not bad. Telling someone about Jesus is good. Asking God to heal someone is good. Every good thing comes from God (James 1:17). So if you feel like God might be prompting you to do something good, even if it's not a word of knowledge from the Lord it's better to obey than to miss an opportunity to see God's glory.

Once I was in a shop I really like. I had been witnessing to the owner over several visits. I had told her that Jesus loved her and that God was good and wanted to bless her and her kids, even in the aftermath of a divorce. I kept telling my wife I was going back to witness, but really it was just an excuse to shop. (Ladies, take notes here—this is a really good excuse to shop.)

So I was in this shop I'd been going to for about a month. On this particular day, an elderly lady came in looking for a t-shirt for her husband. The owner asked her what size she needed, and the lady looked at me and said, "Well, he's a bit big—about his size." Ouch!

Well, this is a classy shop, so the t-shirts are a bit expensive. When the elderly lady found out how much the shirt cost, she said, "Oh, I'm sorry—I can't afford that."

She was handing it back and turning for the door when I heard the Holy Spirit say, *"Buy it for her."* Now, I was still getting over the "big" comment, but onto this the Lord added, *"Buy her the most expensive one."*

"Why?" I asked.

"Because it shows what Jesus is like," God answered.

I thought, *that's all well and good for You—You own the cattle on a thousand hills . . .* But I spoke up and said, "Ma'am, I'll buy it for you."

She was surprised. "Really?" The owner took the lady's hand and led her back to the t-shirts.

"Let her pick out the most expensive one," I told the shop owner.

As they walked to the t-shirts, I heard the owner say, "Do you know what he does? He's a preacher, and he believes that Jesus died for you and rose again—that He wants to give you life to the full and bless you!" She was repeating word for word what I had shared with her over my last few visits.

Now, on the outside I was the picture of James Bond—smooth, totally put together. But on the inside, my kidney was high-fiving my heart, and my heart was high-fiving my lungs. I was going nuts!

So my friend, American Express, paid for the t-shirt, and I told the lady, "There you go, ma'am. I hope he likes it."

"Thank you," she told me.

"No problem," I said with a smile.

"No, no, really—*thank you!*" and she started to cry. Then I started to cry, and the owner started to cry . . . and we didn't even know why we were crying. "You don't understand. My husband is in the hospital down the road. He has a terminal disease, and he just loves t-shirts. He's been so unhappy, and I thought I'd just buy him a t-shirt to cheer him up. I don't even know what made me come into this store, but thank you."

I asked her for her husband's name, and I prayed for him.

This simple act of honoring God's word to me and buying a t-shirt released heaven not only into this lady's life but also into the shopkeeper's life and into mine. It changed the atmosphere.

Change the Atmosphere

The Bible tells the story of a woman of ill repute who changed an atmosphere. She entered the house of a religious leader where Jesus was visiting. When she found Him, she broke open an alabaster jar of perfume worth a year's wage. Then she poured it over His feet.

The whole time, she was crying—great, wet sobs. She washed Jesus' feet with those tears and perfumed them with her most precious possession. Then she wiped His feet with her hair. The sweet smelling fragrance filled the entire room (John 12:3).

She changed the atmosphere.

WHEN WE HONOR GOD'S WORD, WE CHANGE THE ATMOSPHERE.

When we honor God's word, we change the atmosphere. When I bought that t-shirt, the shop's atmosphere changed from a place of buying and selling to a place of heaven. One act of obedience changed lives—the three of us in the shop and the thousands who have heard me share that story.

God wants us to be atmosphere-changers in our world, and He doesn't necessarily need us to be overly "spiritual" about it. This reminds me how God used my mother to change our neighborhood when we moved back to Australia from India.

We lived in a poor area, and no one on the street talked to anyone else. It was a closed-off neighborhood. Well, my mother felt the Lord tell her to send everyone on the street a Christmas card from the Evans family. So she got everyone's name and address and sent all our neighbors Christmas cards. She did the same the next year, and that year we got a few back. The next year she did it again, and we got a heap back.

Before long the whole street was sending each other Christmas cards. Mother started baking things for people, and neighbors who were sick got help and meals. The entire culture of the street changed; the atmosphere changed because my mother obeyed.

It started with a small thing—sending Christmas cards. There's nothing overly spiritual about that, but her obedience opened a door for God to work there.

Honor and Obedience

When God tells you to do something, it isn't enough to respond with lip service. A positive attitude isn't enough—you can agree with the word and even honor it in your heart, but true honor results in action. We must act. We must obey.

Actions as simple as sending Christmas cards, paying for someone's t-shirt, praying for someone, and starting a conference called Planetshakers all hinged on obedience. Without obedience, none of this would have happened. Without obedience, the world won't change.

> WITHOUT OBEDIENCE, EVEN POSITIVE WORDS AND ATTITUDES ARE ONLY GOOD INTENTIONS.

Jesus once told an interesting story about obedience. "A man had two sons, and he came to the first and said, 'Son, go, work today in my vineyard.' He answered and said, 'I will not,' but afterward he regretted it and went. Then he came to the second and said likewise. And he answered and said, 'I go, sir,' but he did not go. Which of the two did the will of his father?" (Matthew 21:28–31 NKJV)

God gives words to us all the time, but who ultimately honors the Father? Those who struggle with a word but finally obey, or those who accept the word but never act on it? Jesus used this story to contrast sinners, who listened to Him and repented, with religious people who listened but refused to repent.

Which will you be? The one who only hears, or the one who hears and obeys? You can let God soften your heart and you can say all the right words, but without obedience, you'll never create the honor synergy that brings inheritance into your life. Without obedience, even positive words and attitudes are only good intentions.

God Honors Obedience

God does miraculous things when people obey. Let me share one recent experience. I was speaking at a conference in New Zealand when God gave me a word that someone's lungs had been scarred and God wanted to bring healing. I found out that a woman with cancer had experienced significant scarring in her lungs from chemotherapy. When she heard me share that word, she claimed it for herself. She said, "That's for me," and stood up—and at that very moment, God healed her lungs. She sent us a praise report after her lungs were tested: the examination showed that the burns on her lungs were completely gone. She acted in obedience and God honored that word.

Another amazing example of obedience happened at our church. A guest speaker, Glen Berteau, visited our church after he had suffered a severe heart attack that required significant surgery. He shared with us how he came out of the surgery with a message on his heart: Devil, Your Request Has Been Denied.

A couple from our church heard this message and had reason to stand on the word he shared when, later in the week, the mother accidentally backed over their two-year-old daughter with an SUV.

Her husband ran out and picked up the little limp form. They rushed into the house and prayed over her. With their baby in their arms, completely unresponsive, they spoke the word they had received earlier in the week. "Devil, your request has been denied!" They prayed for life and stood on God's goodness.

When the father laid his hand on that little girl, it was as though electricity arched through his hand into her small body. She went from lifeless to alive and was conscious for the drive to the hospital. The doctors evaluated her overnight, but while they had expected internal injuries and broken bones at the least, they found only bruises and scrapes from the gravel on the driveway. That next Sunday the little girl sang in our kid's area at church.

Devil, your request was denied!

That miracle came because her parents stood on a word they had received from God.

God has also had me share words with individuals— some of them quite bold. God told me to share a word with a friend who had a conference in England. "You need to plant a church in Manchester," I told him. We were at a very "spiritual" setting—watching cricket—when God just dropped that word in my mind.

He asked me what I meant, and I just said, "You've got a church in Manchester, England, that needs you to start it."

"How do you know?" he asked.

"I just know that God is telling me He wants you to start a church in Manchester," I replied. I was being obedient in saying this to him, because it's a serious matter to speak into someone's life in this manner.

He was an associate pastor at the time and was concerned about what his senior pastor would say. But his pastor released him from his position, and he started a church in Manchester. That church just celebrated its fifth anniversary, and now has over two thousand people in attendance, which for England is enormous! That church is changing the community and making an impact on the people of Manchester—all because God gave a word to an associate pastor who obeyed and stepped out in honor.

The word God shared with me confirmed the Holy Spirit's leading to my friend. He had a choice of honor or cynicism, as we all do.

Friend, Father, and King

There are times in our lives when we relate to God as a friend. In prayer, speaking to Him as a friend can produce wonderful intimacy. There are also times when He relates to us as Father, and the Father relationship speaks of inheritance and blessing. But when we relate to God as King, it is about rule and order. At times, God puts people in our lives who represent each of His different character traits. We should enjoy and honor the friendship, fatherly love, and leadership from those He appoints in our lives.

People may relate to us in any of these three ways. They may relate to us and help us laugh. They may be parents to us and bless us. Or they may be leaders to us who speak direction into our lives or call us to account for things we've done wrong. If we resist their leadership, we work against the flow of blessings in our lives. If we embrace their leadership, we release the flow of blessing.

Receiving individual words and receiving a word given corporately are two different things. When we sit under authority, God sometimes gives directions or instructions to those appointed over us. We always have a choice of whom we submit to, but if you're under someone's leadership and God gives direction through that person, your response is either honor or cynicism. If you feel that person is manipulating or intimidating or controlling—abusing the idea of honor—then you have a choice whether to remain under the authority of that person. If you choose to remain under that authority, you choose to submit to a person God has appointed over you as a type of "king."

> IF WE EMBRACE THEIR LEADERSHIP, WE RELEASE THE FLOW OF BLESSING.

This can also happen much closer to home—not just with our relationship with our pastor. These relationships I'm talking about (friend, father, and king) are figurative in our families as well.

My wife, Sam, and I give a lot of premarital counseling, and she shares with future wives how God instructed her to honor me. She learned early in our marriage that certain things about me drove her crazy! She'd tell me something and I'd say "Okay," but then she'd have to remind me about it again and again— until I'd get upset and ask her to quit talking about it. Sometimes

I still wouldn't get the message, but instead of nagging me, she took it to my "higher authority."

"Father," she prayed, "could you deal with my husband? I need you to change his heart." She could have chosen to get in the way of God dealing with me by nagging me, but she chose to honor me by going to the authority over me. She went to God and asked Him to deal with my hard heart, and He could do something her words never could. He could soften my heart, change it, and bend me to His will for the sake of our lives and our marriage.

God showed her that we can actually become instruments of obstruction. Cynicism will do this in your life—it will be an obstruction to the blessings God wants to pour out. If you don't agree with those appointed to your life, you can leave . . . or you can pray for them, stay in an attitude of honor, and ask God to change their hearts.

> CYNICISM WILL DO THIS IN YOUR LIFE—IT WILL BE AN OBSTRUCTION TO THE BLESSINGS GOD WANTS TO POUR OUT.

Do you feel that blessings have been obstructed in your life? Check yourself—you may have to exchange cynicism for honor in order to release the flow God desires.

Who to Honor

It's one thing to honor those over you when they love you sacrificially and don't try to manipulate. But what do we do when someone in a role of father or king in our lives is off base or abuses the position?

To judge the validity of a word over your life, follow the same rules you use to judge prophecy. Ask if the person is respected in your church community and verify whether the word lines up with God's Word and is confirmed in your spirit. If you have reason to doubt that what a person has shared is of God, you still have a choice to make—whether or not to give that person honor.

If you have doubts about a personal word, you might tell the individual that you honor them and love them but what they have said doesn't agree with what the Lord has shown you. It's good to make sure your words are spoken in the open, in the light, and not shrouded in secrecy. You don't want to be rude or arrogant; you want to have a soft heart and a soft answer (Proverbs 15:1). Ask God for His wisdom and discernment.

> IF YOU WANT TO UNLEASH GOD'S INHERITANCE, YOU WILL HONOR, OBEY, AND ACT UPON THE WORDS HE GIVES YOU.

In a church or corporate setting, you can honor what the pastor says or you can leave that church—if you cannot honor what the pastor says, why stay there? Go someplace where you can honor the pastor.

A few years ago a guest speaker came to a friend's church while he was gone. He was a trustworthy man, a prophet, but my friend didn't know him personally. When he saw my friend's wife and daughter alone at the Sunday night service, he gave them a word that was not correct at all—he thought she was a single mom with a teenage daughter. Nothing he said to them was correct.

Instead of making a fuss about it, my friend's wife remained quiet, but my friend called the speaker's pastor and made him aware of the situation. The pastor then called the speaker, and to his credit, the guy handled it with a proper, humble spirit. It could have been more bizarre, but instead it was handled well and in order. The person in authority over this speaker addressed the problem, and this is how God wants us to handle these things.

We dishonor God if we honor a lie, so if you can't trust the pastor you're under, you'll never receive from that person. If you can't trust, it will be difficult for you to honor. And if you don't honor, you won't receive.

This concept of honoring the word you receive is, at its core, less about receiving words from individuals and more about receiving words from those God has appointed over you—the leaders of your local church. It's important to be under the covering of your church leaders, because they will give an account for your soul (Hebrews 13:17).

So what will you chose? What action will you take when God gives you words from those in "king" or "father" positions in your life? Your cynicism can obstruct what God wants to do in your life. But if you want to unleash God's inheritance, you will honor, obey, and act upon the words He gives you.

Do you want to see the world saved? So do I. It's time to obey what God tells us to do.

CHAPTER 11

MULTIPLICATION EFFECT

My grandfather was saved because a preacher in Wales honored God, stopped in the middle of his sermon, and walked back to the hall to where a young man sat. "Are you saved?" he asked my grandfather, who was seventeen. He was a coalminer and had no future outside of mining coal—until honor entered the picture.

"No," my grandfather answered. But not for long!

At the same time, in Australia, my four-foot tall grandmother sat in a meeting and listened to some guy named Smith Wigglesworth preach. She heard the call to follow Jesus, and she honored the call. Later, Aimee Semple McPherson spoke, and my grandmother honored her message on the baptism in the Holy Spirit. Then, God called her as a missionary to India, and as a young girl in her twenties, she boarded a boat to India to honor God's call on her life.

As I mentioned earlier, my grandfather heard the Lord's call in Wales and got on a boat and headed to the mission field—to India, as it turns out. My grandparents met in India and served there for twenty-five years before coming to Australia. My father was born in India, and he went on to become an incredibly influential man in Australia—both in church and in government. And he, of course, had two sons: my brother and I.

At eighty, my grandmother lay dying. My grandfather, mother, and I all joined hands around her bed, and my grandfather prayed, "Dear Jesus, I thank you for having the honor of serving you. We have given you our very best, and we have no regrets."

When he finished the prayer, my grandmother said goodbye to all her loved ones, even though only three of us were there. When she had gone through a list of all the family members, I said to her, "Grandma, I'll see you in heaven. I wouldn't be serving Jesus if it weren't for you."

We headed out then, and two hours later her last words were, "Oh for the souls of young men and women." Then she died.

Three days later I had the honor of carrying her coffin at her funeral, and as I did so, tears streamed down my face. Now, every time a Planetshakers song plays, every time a person is saved through that ministry, and every time the Holy Spirit moves in one of our meetings, I know it's because my grandma and grandpa honored what God called them to do. My parents also honored God's call on their lives, and because of that direct lineage of honor stretching back to my grandparents, Planetshakers was born. Our conferences have impacted the lives of tens of thousands of young people around the globe—and millions more who have heard our music.

This is a picture of the multiplication effect of honor and a profound example of the power of honor to release a generational blessing.

Abraham's Blessing

God told Abraham to count the stars in the sky. That was to be the number of his inheritance. But years after he received the promise, Abraham still didn't have one descendant. How could God give him a vision for billions of descendants when he didn't even have one? Truly Abraham's promise was a generational one, for when God said that He would bless him and make him a great nation, that promise was not fulfilled solely with Isaacs' birth.

Isaac honored the promise God had given to Abraham, and God gave Isaac two sons. This was addition. Jacob then honored the promise from Abraham that was on his father, Isaac, and the promise went from addition to multiplication. Jacob had twelve sons, and the entire Jewish nation descended from his line. We count Abraham as the father of our Christian faith, and the billions of Christians who are alive right now are proof of God's faithfulness to give Abraham his full inheritance.

> *ABRAHAM'S PROMISE WAS A GENERATIONAL ONE, FOR WHEN GOD SAID THAT HE WOULD BLESS HIM AND MAKE HIM A GREAT NATION, THAT PROMISE WAS NOT FULFILLED SOLELY WITH ISAACS' BIRTH.*

Generational Blessings

From the time of Abraham until now, we can see billions of children of the promise. How did that blessing come? Through honor—each generation honored the promise from the previous generation. Even though some generations dropped it, someone always picked up the promise.

Years ago when I began to work in ministry, a youth group in Australia with fifty kids was considered big—it was massive. Now, thirty years later, a big youth group in Australia is two thousand kids! Many youth groups have fifty, and in fact that would be considered a small group now. Plenty have more than five hundred kids! I feel that a generational blessing came when succeeding generations honored what God was doing in Australia among the youth. We've been blessed to participate in this and to see true multiplication through Planetshakers.

What kind of view do you have? Do you see one month down the road? Maybe you plan a year ahead? What about ten? Some people feel that a generation is forty to fifty years, and I believe we should have the sort of generational viewpoint that measures the outworking of promises in the timeframe of an entire generation. How would it influence your choices if you looked fifty years down the line? What about one hundred? You would make choices with a generational mindset, and you would honor and teach your children to honor with that in mind.

Many generations have felt that Jesus Christ was coming back during their lifetimes. Back in the sixties and seventies, believers were sure Jesus was returning at any moment. As a result, too many churches and denominations stopped strategizing for the future and became political and resistant, due to their inability to stay fresh and relevant. Why? Because we didn't think generationally.

Have you ever wondered how you can change a culture? You get them to change their ideologies, which then influences their beliefs. Our beliefs change our behavior, which in turn alters our lifestyle. Altered lifestyles become strongholds. That's how you transform a nation. We can recognize that process and see the potential of the church to change the ideologies of our day, or we can cry and whine when the world thinks more long-term than we do and influences our culture in ways that are not kingdom-focused.

I once heard about John Calvin's visit to Geneva. At the time, Geneva was known for prostitution and corruption. It was the slum of Europe, but Calvin decided to preach the gospel there and release the kingdom through excellence in every part of society. That was roughly two hundred years ago, and because he had a generational view, he changed the culture of the city. It's now known for excellence, with brands like Rolex calling it home, as well as organizations like the Red Cross. Don't forget the Geneva Convention, written by Henry Dunant, a devout Calvinist, and the World Bank. Instead of being a place of prostitution and corruption, it's now known for peace, prosperity, and integrity.

What happened? Kingdom influence came into the society, and because of a long-term view, God worked through men to change a culture.

> *HONOR IS THE CONNECTIVE TISSUE BETWEEN GENERATIONS. IT'S WHAT GIVES CONNECTION AND CONTINUITY AMONG GENERATIONS OF GOD'S PEOPLE.*

God isn't influenced by time—He's the Alpha and Omega, the Beginning and the End—so when He looks at us, He doesn't just think of today. He looks at tomorrow, and the generation after that, and the generation after that. He looks hundreds and even thousands of years down the line—just look at the lineage of Jesus, both before King David and after!

Honor is the connective tissue between generations. It's what gives connection and continuity among generations of God's people. In the Bible, God describes Himself as the God of Abraham, Isaac, and Jacob. Three generations. He doesn't describe Himself as the God of Abraham, Moses, and Elijah. Three generations establish a kingdom footprint—it can't be done in one generation. And while God sees all of time, and He is the God of Abraham, Moses, and Elijah, He understands how a multigenerational view establishes His kingdom on earth through us, His human vessels.

It's true that our enemy targets all of us, but I feel he focuses especially on the third generation, because the third generation brings multiplication.

It's easy to get caught up on the short-term, shallow view our culture has on life. At best, we may think in terms of our generation and influence—roughly forty years, because that's generally our most productive season. But what would happen if every Christian thought in terms of multiple generations like God does?

Pass on the Inheritance and Blessing

My grandfather was in his late eighties and blind when he told me that he wanted to continue to learn the Word. I said, "What do you mean, 'learn the Word'? You already know the Word, Grandpa!" He told me he wanted to learn to read braille! I told him that he could listen to the Bible, but he said that wasn't enough—he wanted to read it for himself. So at eighty-eight years of age, he learned braille so he could read and study the Bible!

SOMETHING SUPERNATURAL COMES WHEN YOU HONOR WHAT GOD HAS DONE IN THE PREVIOUS GENERATION AND WHAT HE WILL DO IN FUTURE GENERATIONS.

My grandfather was truly an amazing man, though for the longest time, he didn't progress beyond our church's youth group! He still came to youth services into his late eighties, even though they were not his style. Why? He wanted to honor not just his son's generation but his grandson's generation—and beyond! He came to the services because he loved the life and wanted to be part of the energy of younger people. The music wasn't his style; but the future was. So he honored us by being there and saying, "yes and amen" to what was going on in our generation.

The devil knows that if he separates generations, he separates the passing of inheritance and blessing. Something supernatural comes when you honor what God has done in the previous generation and what He will do in future generations. This is one of the reasons God gives us children in the first place, because children make us change with them. Without that change, we stagnate and become cynical of the next generation.

My grandparents were missionaries in India who touched many lives, but it was up to my father to honor what the Lord had done through them. My brother and I, in turn, honored what God did through our grandparents and our father, and the multiplication effect has allowed ministry far beyond anything our grandfather ever dreamed. In a sense, his influence continues to touch millions even though he's no longer alive. Why? Because of honor.

What Stops Generations

The devil uses many devices to halt the torch of God's Word and keep it from being passed to another generation. He uses superficial differences like style, but the attitudes often come back to cynicism. Styles change, and moves of God ebb and flow; a generation that stops moving and growing is a generation that stops multiplying. Our roles change, and we must honor the generation that has come before and what God did in it while also honoring the generation that comes after and what God is doing in it.

If the devil can get you to discount what a generation has done in the past or in the present, on the grounds of something as simple as style or taste, he can often get you to quit honoring. If he can do that, he can separate generations and prevent the power of multiplication from bringing kingdom influence.

My role as a son to my father is very different to my role as father to my children. My father had to go through that same change of roles as he grew up under my grandfather's ministry. When I came into the world, my father's father became a grandfather—his role changed. So did my father's. When you are a father, God gives you grace for that time, the same way He gives you grace to be a grandfather or a son. We have different roles in different seasons, and at one point my grandfather was no longer able to operate as a father only. He was not my father, he was my grandfather, and I honored and respected him for who he was to our family. But this role was different to that of my father, in the same way that my role will one day change when my children have kids.

> A SON'S JOB IS TO PROVIDE STRENGTH AND ENERGY, A FATHER'S JOB IS TO DRIVE, AND A GRANDFATHER'S JOB IS TO PROVIDE WISDOM.

We can honor the younger generation by recognizing their energy and enthusiasm. Instead of complaining about their style, which may not be our taste, we must recognize that God is using it to touch them and we can honor that. Younger people can honor the previous generation by taking advantage of their experience and wisdom. Instead of complaining that the older generation is out of touch, the younger generation can gain perspective on how things have changed—for better or worse.

I like to look at it like this: A son's job is to provide strength and energy, a father's job is to drive, and a grandfather's job is to provide wisdom. Previous generations provide history and context, and outside of context, grandchildren don't understand what they're living for. Without drive and direction, a family is adrift, so without a father, young people spend their energy

without direction, experience, or wisdom. They may have
plenty of drive, but no one is directing that drive so they don't
know where they're going!

We're not each doing our own thing in time and space.
Someone has come before, and someone will come after.
Each brings something unique, and our roles change as the
generations pass.

New Mountains to Conquer

My grandfather was such a testimony to me, for as he aged and
his role changed, he still honored. He continued to grow and do
new things. When he was in his seventies, He had an encounter
with God and wrote a song—he'd never written a song in his
life! He said there were things that had bothered him all his
life that he decided to let go. He decided he was not too old
to change.

I was still a youth leader when he came to me and said,
"Russell, God has told me to plant a church in the Outback of
Australia." You have to understand that at this point he couldn't
see! Imagine, a blind preacher planting a church in the Outback
of Australia!

He wanted me to find a young person who would travel
with him for a month in order to start a church. Well I didn't
shoot down his idea, but I also didn't exert myself to find that
helper. So he came to me the next week and said, "Have you
found that young person yet?"

He bothered me like that for two months! After that, he
came to me and told me he had found his own young person. He

left the next week on a little plane, led by the hand to knock on every door in this small neighborhood in the Outback. He told everyone he was starting a church the next week and invited them to come, and fifty people came to that first service! He stayed the full month and then told my father he was coming home and that my dad needed to find a pastor for this church.

I regret not acting in honor to find someone to take my grandfather into the Outback of Australia, but his example serves as an inspiration not to lose my fire in my older years. From the day I was born, until the day I die, I want to be young at heart. I want to think generationally like my grandfather did, because I don't want the devil to stop the power of honor to multiply over generations.

You can't change the date on your birth certificate, but you can change your attitude. You choose whether or not to honor the generations that have come before and the generations that will follow. Will you be like my grandfather, who conquered new mountains into his twilight years, who embraced changing roles and continued to honor what God was doing? Or will you let cynicism break the connective flow of honor between generations? As for me, I choose honor.

CHAPTER 12

RELEASING MIRACLES

We have explored the powerful and miraculous life of Jesus as He flowed in honor with His Father and the might of the Holy Spirit. So what prevented Him from doing mighty miracles? The lack of honor. But I would like to look at it another way, for even more subtle than dishonor is something you may not think of as a miracle killer—familiarity.

You've probably heard the phrase "familiarity breeds contempt," so becoming overly familiar and unappreciative is a sure way to lose awe. Awe, in fact, is our single best weapon against familiarity.

I've attended too many funerals where people said they wished they had said something to their departed loved one before he or she died. Why didn't they say what was so important when that person lived? Because they accepted familiarity. They became complacent—and it obstructed something important from passing between them.

How many church services take place around the world where the people hear the Word (or words) and cynically think, "Well, I've heard this before"? How many hearts have grown hard with familiarity and cynicism?

God desires to give us a heart of flesh, a soft heart. And nothing breaks through a hard heart like awe.

In the second chapter of the book of Acts, we read that the power of the Holy Spirit came upon the disciples. Peter delivered an inspired message, and many people believed in Jesus. They devoted themselves to the apostles' teaching, fellowship, sharing meals together, and prayer. Into that mix, "A deep sense of awe came over them all, and the apostles performed many miraculous signs and wonders" (Acts 2:43 NLT).

> WE TEND TO THINK OF MIRACLES AS A SUPERNATURAL EVENT, BUT I'VE FOUND THAT MIRACLES ALSO HAPPEN IN PRACTICAL WAYS.

The sense of awe came over them first, and the miracles came after. When Jesus went to His hometown, the townsfolk had no awe of Him; they only had familiarity. Where there is awe and honor, miracles happen in every aspect of life.

Practical Miracles

We tend to think of miracles as a supernatural event, but I've found that miracles also happen in practical ways. Our church has sponsored thousands and thousands of children in Africa and Asia, and when we honor by giving to them, it creates miracles in their lives. Even though we can become familiar in our giving, such as sponsoring a child long-term, that child and the workers who care for that child will still receive our gifts with great awe and treat the giver with great honor, thereby multiplying the benefit of that gift in their lives.

> *WHEN WE HONOR WHAT THE HOLY SPIRIT IS DOING, WE SET HIM FREE TO WORK IN OUR LIVES AND THE LIVES OF OTHERS.*

I remember one time, we helped a school that had suffered a lot of violence by providing an anti-bullying program. Our church came in and did a makeover, with students helping us. They invested in making their school more beautiful, and we have upheld a commitment to preventing bullying so it doesn't get bad again. We honored that school by serving those kids, and I believe that released practical miracles that helped the students take on the responsibility of keeping their school beautiful, clean, and safe.

Spiritual Miracles

Whenever you honor the Holy Spirit, whenever you honor what Jesus has said—both in the Bible and to you personally—you release miracles. As we have freely received, the culture of our kingdom is that we give. The mandate of our kingdom is to heal the sick, free the captives, cast out devils, and raise what is dead back to life.

Honor releases miracles like little bits of heaven come down to us. When we honor what the Holy Spirit is doing, we set Him free to work in our lives and the lives of others. I call this creating an atmosphere for miracles.

In contrast, cynicism creates an atmosphere that lowers the expectation for miracles to the level of the cynic. Want miracles to happen? Practice honor. Want nothing to happen? Be cynical.

Honor creates a space in the natural for the supernatural to operate. It lets a bit of heaven break through. Jesus carried honor with Him, and He didn't permit people to change that atmosphere. Remember, He was unable to do mighty works in His hometown. In the story where Jesus healed the daughter of Jairus, we read that He kicked everyone out of Jairus' home except for the parents, Peter, James, and John. Why? When Jesus gave a word: "The child is not dead, but sleeping" (Mark 5:39 NKJV), the people took a break from their supposedly intense grief to laugh at Him.

When you are clinging to faith for a miracle, when Jesus has told you not to be afraid but to believe in Him, kick out anything that promotes dishonor or cynicism. Jesus kicked out all the mocking cynics, and He brought into the little girl's room only those who would honor what He said.

In the West we rely a great deal on traditional medicine, but in parts of the world where people don't have access to those resources, they often trust God a great deal more. When I was in India, I recognized that the country had a different spiritual climate. They didn't have abundant medical resources, so they trusted and honored God. Now, I do believe that physicians and medicine do a great deal of healing, but we must be careful not to be cynical about the spiritual and only believe in medicine.

While I was in India, we prayed for sick people who came forward to receive from God. Because of the atmosphere there, people were more inclined to honor what the Lord was doing. They asked me to lay hands upon every sick person to receive healing, and there were thousands! We prayed, and the Lord opened deaf ears—at least two hundred of them! He moved in many mighty ways.

However, when I returned to Australia, the same atmosphere for healing wasn't there. Though I had the same desire for God to heal, the people weren't able to receive healing because the atmosphere was different. Since beginning our church, I've actively sought to create an atmosphere that is open to the miracles of God. We believe strongly in God's power to heal—and that's exactly what happens. Does everyone get healed? No. But we have an atmosphere of honor and faith, so we have the necessary currency of heaven.

Instead of begging, "Please, God," we say, "Thank you, God!"

Something to Work With

We've said that it's important for faith and honor to work together as the currency of heaven, and we've discussed how important action is. But when we talk about miracles, we must give the Holy Spirit something to work with.

We see a great example of this when Jesus fed the five thousand. The disciples told Him the people were hungry and asked Him to send them away, but what did Jesus do? He told

His disciples to feed them! He gave a word. Would the disciples honor it?

I'm not sure how much honor they had when they brought a little boy's lunch to Jesus, but they did bring it. Now, when I was a little kid, my mom used to tell me not to share my lunch but to eat it. This little boy shared his lunch with over 5,000 people! He gave his lunch to Jesus.

And that was enough.

From a few loaves of bread and two small fish, Jesus worked a mighty miracle that fed thousands temporarily and impacted many more for a lifetime. It started with something small, but in the economy of heaven, faith is measured in grains like mustard seeds.

What will you bring for the Lord to work with? Your time? Your money? Your obedience? Sometimes we don't have much to work with, but a little is enough.

When Jesus walked on the water to the disciples, Peter didn't have much to offer—just a little bit of faith. But when Jesus gave him a word, "Come," he responded in honor. What did he receive? Peter *walked on water* with Jesus.

Some people may say that Peter sank in the water, but I like to point out that for a time he walked on water just like the Son of God! Jesus certainly wasn't going to sink, so Peter was safer sinking near Jesus then sitting in the boat.

When you take what you have in your hands and place it in God's hands, the focus is no longer on what you have in your hands—it's about Him having *you* in *His* hands. When you don't honor with what you have, when you're cynical, remember what you have: nothing.

Honor puts you, and what you have, in the hands of Jesus. Cynicism leaves you alone with what you have in your hands. So, whose hands are you in?

Intimacy, Not Familiarity

At the beginning of this chapter, I warned that familiarity can be a miracle killer, and I want to return to this for just a moment to ensure something is clear. The reason familiarity breeds contempt is that we begin to take things for granted. We forget how special something or someone is.

> HONOR PUTS YOU, AND WHAT YOU HAVE, IN THE HANDS OF JESUS. CYNICISM LEAVES YOU ALONE WITH WHAT YOU HAVE IN YOUR HANDS.

I remember when my friend first got an iPhone. I watched in awe as he browsed the web, brought up pictures of a particular item he wanted to buy, and effortlessly returned emails. When I first got one, I enjoyed how well it worked, how it enhanced my productivity. I was still impressed, but the awe factor wasn't as strong. After I had one for a time and I used it every day for mundane things, the awe and respect for what it could do faded with familiarity.

This is a trite example, but it helps us consider the danger of becoming familiar with miracles. Imagine the moves of God becoming commonplace, expected, and familiar . . . like my shiny new iPhone.

So what keeps us from becoming overly familiar with the things of God?

Awe. And what brings awe? Staying intimate with the Lord. When you're intimate with God, when you honor His greatness, "familiarity" with His infinite goodness, mercy, and power is impossible.

After being on the mountain and receiving the Ten Commandments, Moses' face glowed so much he had to wear a veil. God couldn't show Himself fully to Elijah but let him see only His back—otherwise the prophet would have *died*.

It's impossible to grow "familiar" with a God who is so holy that simply *looking* upon Him brings death to unrighteous human beings.

If you get close to God, intimate with God, you won't become familiar with His mighty power—you will grow from glory to glory. When my kids were little, we played hide and seek. Naturally, when they were very small, I hid where I was easy to find: behind the couch with part of me hanging out. They found me easily and laughed and squealed. But as they grew older, I hid a little better so that finding me was more of a challenge—and a reward.

WE THINK SIGNS AND WONDERS BRING AWE, BUT AWE OF GOD ALLOWS HIM TO MOVE WITH SIGNS AND WONDERS.

I didn't hide more carefully to show them up or to show them who was better at hide and seek. I did it so they wouldn't become familiar with the game. This is what God is like: the more mature you are, the more He hides His deeper mysteries. He urges you to go deeper, not to settle for the shallow and mundane.

Growing more intimate with God won't result in familiarity; it will result in intrigue, fascination, and hunger for more and more of Him.

Do you recall what I said at the end of chapter eight—that what you're intimate with is what you produce? Intimacy with the moves of God, and not with God Himself, may seem like a good thing, but over time it can diminish your awe of Him. Only intimacy with God Himself prevents familiarity and breathes awe into your relationship with Him.

We think signs and wonders bring awe, but awe of God allows Him to move with signs and wonders. Intimacy with God inspires awe in us as He reveals new facets of His goodness and character. Intimacy with Him shows the depth and extent of His promises for your life.

Familiarity kills miracles, but intimacy births *promises*.

CHAPTER 13

RELEASE THE COMMANDED BLESSING

Wherever people practice the principle of honor, unity results. And whenever people experience unity and protect it, God releases a "commanded blessing." This principle comes from a rich Bible passage, Psalm 133:

> Behold, how good and how pleasant it is for brethren to dwell together in unity! It is like the precious oil upon the head, running down on the beard, the beard of Aaron, running down on the edge of his garments. It is like the dew of Hermon, descending upon the mountains of Zion; for there the LORD commanded the blessing—life forevermore. (Psalm 133:1–3 NKJV)

To command means to charge, to give orders, or to ordain. When God commands a blessing over our lives, nothing can stop it. As we've discussed since the first chapter, honor creates unity, as it does in the Godhead, and we read here that unity is the vehicle for God's commanded blessing.

Wouldn't you like to have God command a blessing over you? Psalm 133 shows that this is directly tied to unity, which David so beautifully describes as being like oil.

When things are in unity, they are in harmony. As a musician I find it easy to think in terms of notes that blend pleasantly. When there is disunity, there is discord—which is not pleasant. As the body of Christ, we must seek to work in harmony, because the end results are pleasant to God and to us. But what happens when we dishonor?

Remove the "Dis" From Your Life

God is always able to bless us, but we aren't always able to receive the blessing. Did you know that discord and disunity prevent us from receiving God's blessings? When I honor those appointed over me, my peers, and those to whom I minister, everything is in order.

Dishonor brings discord and, even more, I believe dishonor actually honors the devil. When we fear, we believe what he says more than what God says. Think about what fear really is—it's essentially faith that the devil's words are true and God's words are not true.

The prefix *dis-* means "opposed to," so when we have dishonor in our lives, we oppose the things of God. This causes disruption in our lives, distrust, and even destruction. Honor holds it all together; it creates unity. Dishonor, then, is the exact opposite.

Did you know that discord and disunity prevent us from receiving God's blessings?

In a previous chapter I mentioned how important it is for each generation to honor older generations and younger generations. But we think we need to understand other generations and give our approval for the things they do in order for the body of Christ to be in unity. That's not true—we need to honor in order for things to be in unity.

We'll never understand everything. We don't understand everything God is doing in our own generation, let alone other generations! If we wait to understand before we honor, we'll never have a complete picture—or unity.

Unity Among Generations

I love it when my congregation bring their Bibles to church, but these days more and more people use their mobile devices to read the Bible. So if you read the Bible on your phone, does that mean you should have your phone out at church?

If a speaker from a previous generation came to our church and didn't recognize that people were reading their Bibles on their phones, he might think they were dishonoring him, when in fact they were actively reading and participating with the Word. He might not understand the appeal of reading the Bible on a small electronic screen, but that doesn't make it wrong.

However, that same speaker from a previous generation might help us all to recognize that too much use of social media and not enough face-to-face contact with real people isn't healthy. His experience can put our need for face time in context, so we must honor him as well.

When we honor him, we recognize that we may need to resist certain cultural trends that aren't healthy. When he honors the next generation's use of technology to read the Word, this releases blessings rather than obstructing them. Honor flowing in both directions promotes unity and creates synergy.

I was recently in Israel, and while its culture is quite secular, the Jewish religious background is still so strong that they honor the Sabbath even in their secular culture. In order to prevent Jews from doing "work," they keep the elevators on automatic on the Sabbath, stopping at every floor, so that no one has to push a button!

It's interesting that before Israel was established as a country after World War II, relatively few Jews used Hebrew as their primary language. After the war, however, Jewish people came from all over Europe and beyond, seeking to return to their ancient homeland. With them, they brought a variety of languages from their cultures. Though many of them had maintained elements of the Jewish culture, scattered though they were, they had a generational understanding of Hebrew but didn't use it extensively outside of its religious context. Because of the Jews' honor for the Torah and their faith, early Israeli leaders were able to establish Hebrew as the official language— even if it meant everyone had to attend Hebrew school!

Honoring their heritage enabled them to hold together in unity as a culture despite long periods of captivity and dispersion. This left the Jews, alone among ancient people groups, with their culture and faith still intact. They tapped this honor across generations to create unity among diverse immigrants from a wide variety of countries. Their unity as a nation has enabled God to bless them even in modern times, despite being small and surrounded by enemies.

Come Together

Paul gives us useful instructions on unity in the book of Philippians:

> Therefore if you have any encouragement from being united with Christ, if any comfort from his love, if any common sharing in the Spirit, if any tenderness and compassion, then make my joy complete by being like-minded, having the same love, being one in spirit and of one mind. Do nothing out of selfish ambition or vain conceit. Rather, in humility value others above yourselves, not looking to your own interests but each of you to the interests of the others. (Philippians 2:1–4)

How can people from different backgrounds, upbringings, and cultures be of one spirit and one mind with other believers? The answer is that we don't operate in the culture of our upbringing and background; we operate in the culture of heaven. When we become new in Christ, we come into relationship with

Him—and with one another. God adopts us all, making us heirs of salvation through Christ, and we make conscious choices to embrace this new heritage when we honor one another.

The result is unity.

When we dishonor each other, we fail to look for the unseen gifts and the presence of God in each other. When we do things out of selfish ambition or vain conceit, we deny the connective tissue that binds us together across the span of generations.

> HUMILITY DOESN'T MEAN YOU PUT YOURSELF DOWN; IT MEANS YOU DON'T THINK ABOUT YOURSELF AT ALL. YOU SEE YOURSELF THROUGH CHRIST.

Remember when we talked about seeing yourself as you ought to? That is where humility and valuing others above yourself comes into play. Humility doesn't mean you put yourself down; it means you don't think about yourself at all. You see yourself through Christ. That view reveals you are one with a body composed of many parts, each with unique value. When we put weight on that value, we show the body honor.

Then honor creates unity, which releases the blessings God has commanded for His people.

Unity Doesn't Mean Being Faceless

Sometimes, people who misunderstand the concept of honor fear that honoring others will turn them into robots. In actuality, nothing could be further from the truth. Honor is not the absence of sharing, communication, and free will. Mutual honor is shared in every direction, so no one is disrespected or left voiceless. No one's needs are ignored.

In a family where there is honor, there is good communication. Family members who honor one another share freely. God made us members of His family and honored us so much more than we deserve. He didn't create us to be robots, and He wants us to partake of all the blessings inherent in being in His family.

> EVERYTHING GOD DOES, HE DOES IN ORDER.

Some people think that showing honor to others will squash their personality. If anything, true honor means that being a silent, robotic person is dishonoring. By not sharing, you withhold your gifts from the body.

Honor promotes good communication within the family—whether the family of God or your own family. Now, as we discussed with receiving words, our goal is to communicate with honor and in order. We can share our perspectives, as long as we are willing to say, "I don't really understand, but I honor you anyway." Returning that honor means we listen to what others have to say and we respect their perspective.

The Order of Anointing

I've mentioned briefly another component of honor—order. Everything God does, He does in order. In fact, there's a right order to everything He created.

In Psalm 133, David described the anointing oil being poured on Aaron's head. Notice that it started at the top of his head and flowed onto the rest of his body. David gives us an image of holy anointing that flows from the head onto the body. This is a picture of our relationship under our head, Christ, and under those He has appointed over us. We are under their covering. When every part of the body is in proper order under the head, the anointing flows from the head and covers all of the body.

However, what would happen to Aaron's arms if he held them out from his body? They would not be covered in the flowing oil. This is a picture of what happens when we are out of order in the body of Christ. Dishonor separates us from the anointing.

Communication is vital in a physical body. If your hand didn't communicate with your brain when you touched a hot stove, you wouldn't realize you were being burned. However, where do the hands' orders come from? They come from the head. We each have a function in the body of Christ and communication is important within His body. If a military unit doesn't communicate, the battle can be lost. If a band doesn't communicate, some musicians will be out of order and there will be discord.

During our Planetshakers Awakenings, there are times in our worship when we spontaneously make a key change in a song. The band director tells the band members we're going up a key at the end of the chorus. If the director doesn't communicate with the band and they don't make the key change together, the sound loses its positive impact—in fact, the impact is decidedly negative!

At Planetshakers, we're blessed to have amazing musicians. But even with their individual greatness, they have to work together or the power of the moment is lost. One time, we planned to do a key change and build up to a crescendo that would take the worship to another level. But something happened in the communication—either people were distracted or couldn't hear or were so lost in worship they didn't register with the plan. When the song leader called for a key change, some of the band members didn't respond. The band wasn't in unity, which distracted the worshipers and stopped the momentum of the moment.

You're not by yourself in this walk of faith. You're part of a unit, and lack of unity can stop the flow that God desires to take you to the next level.

All authority comes from God and proceeds on down through those He has placed in leadership. He created order, and He created the orderly process by which authority and anointing proceed down from Christ Jesus, the head of the body.

People who complain and point out problems may think that their criticism benefits their situation. What they don't understand is that instead of voicing criticism, they should use their words to create solutions. When we bring our gifts, experiences, and perspectives to the table as part of a solution, we contribute to our families, our jobs, and the body of Christ.

WHEN WE BRING OUR GIFTS, EXPERIENCES, AND PERSPECTIVES TO THE TABLE AS PART OF A SOLUTION, WE CONTRIBUTE TO OUR FAMILIES, OUR JOBS, AND THE BODY OF CHRIST.

As the earthly head of my local chapter of the body of Christ, there are times when I am friend, father, or king. There are times when my position is one of a peer and I share openly with others. But there are times when their answer to me is simply, "Yes, Pastor." Those are the times when I instruct people about something important or share a word from the pulpit.

There are times when God speaks to us as a friend. There are times when He blesses us like a Father, and times when our only answer is, "Yes, Sir." We are His sons and daughters, and we may speak freely and approach His throne boldly (Hebrews 4:16), but we do so with awe and respect and honor.

Friendship is honoring each other relationally, fatherhood is honoring from a family perspective, and honoring God's Lordship is about *order* and how we function as members of the body of Christ. Clear communication helps honor to work, because it isn't dishonoring to ask in order to understand. But the key to how we interact is humility of spirit—when we communicate with a humble spirit, we relate to one another with honor.

The unity that results is like the precious oil of anointing God wants to pour over Christ's body—the anointing that will bring His commanded blessings into our lives.

KINGDOM OF ORDER

I was speaking in England on one occasion when I heard myself say, "Honor doesn't work if the order isn't right." I hadn't said that before, and it wasn't in my notes. Where had that thought come from? When I make statements like that out of nowhere, I've learned that it's something God is giving me in the moment. I later sat down to study what God has to say about order.

God's kingdom is a kingdom of order. His kingdom is built on order, and the Bible is full of direct and indirect references to the order in which God operates and through which He created the world.

In Genesis, God gave Adam the mandate to be fruitful, multiply, replenish, subdue, and have dominion—there was a definite order there. As I've mentioned from the beginning of this book, there is an order in the Godhead of Father, Son, and

Holy Spirit. The Holy Spirit reveals the Son, who reveals the Father. There is an order. Our families have an order, and so do church services.

God created order in every aspect of our universe, from subatomic particles to the largest institutions. What we must grasp is that honor and order are both necessary for fruitfulness.

The Order of Fruitfulness

The devil will try to attack two things in a person's life or in an organization—honor and order. Have you ever seen an organization that is well organized but has no honor? It seems mired in its own bureaucracy. What about people who seem to honor and respect everyone but have no order? A bit more fruitfulness can come from that, because God can use anyone, but true honor operates in order.

God lays out the foundations of order and proclaims that He is a God of honor from the very beginning. In the first chapter of Genesis we read that God said, "Let us make mankind in our image . . . so that they may rule over the fish in the sea and the birds in the sky, over the livestock and all the wild animals, and over all the creatures that move along the ground" (Genesis 1:26). Notice His order from the start: God, humans, animals.

THE DEVIL WILL TRY TO ATTACK TWO THINGS IN A PERSON'S LIFE OR IN AN ORGANIZATION— HONOR AND ORDER.

As soon as God created in this orderly fashion, He blessed mankind and said, "Be fruitful and multiply; fill the earth and subdue it; have dominion over the fish of the sea, over the birds of the air, and over every living thing that moves on the earth" (Genesis 1:28 NKJV). So God created mankind to be under Him, and then He gave us instructions to be fruitful, multiply, subdue, and have dominion.

God's orders are for us to multiply the gifts He has given us and to take them into areas that don't have those blessings. We are to replenish with that fruitfulness, and when we have saturated an area with blessing, our fruitfulness will subdue that area and give the kingdom dominion in that part of the earth.

Not so long ago, some shortsighted people interpreted this to be a mandate to strip an area of its natural resources and irresponsibly move on to decimate another area. I don't believe this is what the Lord meant at all. To a world with only two human beings, this was God's commission to Adam and Eve— have lots of little kids to fill up My kingdom on earth. Now, there are people everywhere, and this is a spiritual mandate for Christians—use your gifts to create disciples and fill up the earth with people who follow Jesus.

This is why the enemy will try to attack your fruitfulness and the multiplication of your gifts. That is why he attacks things like our rest, our hearts, our minds, and our unity. He wants to get us out of order.

The Process of Fruitfulness

I first read about the process of fruitfulness in Tudor Bismark's book *The Order of the Kingdom*.[5] He explains that fruitfulness in

---

5   Tudor Bismark, *The Order of the Kingdom* (Maitland, FL: Xulon Press, 2012).

God's kingdom is like taking spiritual fruitfulness into areas of life (physical, spiritual social, relational, geographical, cultural etc.) that are unfruitful, replenishing those areas, subduing them, and ultimately achieving kingdom dominion in those areas. Using our gifts to apply our fruitfulness to someone else's fruitlessness is the essence of living a fruitful life and expanding the kingdom of God in our areas of influence.

When we honor our gifts and talents, as well as those of others, our service creates credibility. Credibility then creates influence, and our influence creates an atmosphere. Atmospheres change cultures, and a culture of growth produces seed that bears fruit. Without activating your gift by honoring it, or without someone releasing your gift by honoring you, that process of order cannot start, which denies the earth your fruitfulness.

> ATMOSPHERES CHANGE CULTURES, AND A CULTURE OF GROWTH PRODUCES SEED THAT BEARS FRUIT.

Serving with our gifts brings credibility, influence, and authority, but when we honor something that is out of order or we don't welcome order in the use of our gifts, the result is disorder and discord.

So let's say God has given you a gift, such as musical talent. When you use that talent to serve Him, He causes it to be fruitful and multiply by blessing the people who hear it. Doing that in order means that you may submit your gift to the direction of a creative pastor, and in that context your musical gift may be able to bless an entire congregation of people.

The order is so important. Let's say you don't have a gift for music, but you try to sing anyway. We've all seen a lot of that on TV! The fruit and credibility that a true gift would have created will not manifest because there is no gift to sing. So, on our worship teams at church, we need to consider whether a person carries the necessary gift and anointing. If we make someone a worship leader who has the desire to sing but has no gift, we are operating out of order because they have no musical gift or anointing, and the discordant results will not bless anyone.

Your service and your gift will produce credibility when you operate in order. I've seen people who started their service as janitors and followed the process of order and fruitfulness into positions of leadership. Many people want to lead and be heard by a crowd, but that requires credibility, which won't come without service, gifts, and character. Focusing too much on character and forgetting gifts is out of order, but so is focusing on gifts and forgetting character. Forgetting one or the other will not produce credibility.

His Will on Earth

How do we learn about order? Jesus understood the origin of all order: "Everything you see me do, I do on behalf of my Father," He said (John 10:37–38). Look at how He taught us to pray: "Our Father in heaven, hallowed be your name, your kingdom come, your will be done, on earth as it is in heaven" (Matthew 6:9–10).

It all starts with God. It's all about the Father's will on earth. A proverb says that as we think, so we are (Proverbs 23:7). So if you're thinking is incorrect about God's kingdom and order, then your worldview will be incorrect. You will ask for the wrong things, and therefore your ability to receive will be affected.

You have to honor the way of the King if you want to participate in His kingdom. God's order says, "Forgive so that you may be forgiven." Our fleshly order says, "You hurt me, so I am going to hurt you back." Which of these orders will bear fruit? The answer is they will both bear fruit—but one will not have the kind of fruit you want!

It seems harsh for God not to forgive and hear our prayers if we don't forgive those who have hurt us. Some people have been badly hurt, and to a mind that hasn't been transformed it seems like that order is reversed—a hurt person should be forgiven and then in turn forgive.

> YOU HAVE TO HONOR THE WAY OF THE KING IF YOU WANT TO PARTICIPATE IN HIS KINGDOM.

I asked God about this in prayer, and I felt that He said to me, "What pleases Me? Faith. Without faith, it is impossible to please Me (Hebrews 11:6). If someone has not forgiven, is he coming to me in faith? No. So can I respond to his prayers? He is out of order, and it obstructs the answers to the prayers he is requesting." It's not that God doesn't want to respond, but when we're not in order we're out of position to receive.

I once appointed a young man who was a little lazy to a position in our youth group. He was the assistant youth pastor, but his behavior quickly frustrated our youth pastor. The youth pastor, in turn, told other people how frustrated he was with his assistant. This was out of order.

When I found out about it, I called the youth pastor and the assistant into my office to discuss the situation. I asked the youth pastor what his problem was with his assistant, and he beat around the bush until I pointedly asked him to tell me what he had been telling other people—but now in front of this assistant. Finally a statement came out: "He's lazy. He doesn't help with packing up."

We processed through this together, and at the end I asked them both, "Who appointed this young man as your assistant?" They both answered that I had. I then asked, "Who is the one ultimately responsible for his performance?" Again, they both answered that it was my responsibility.

Here is a case where I was in the role of a father, because even though the performance issue was with the assistant, the disorder issue was with both of them. I asked him, "Why are you telling other people about this man's performance instead of addressing him directly or talking to the one who appointed him? You are out of order." The assistant was out of order for not respecting the youth pastor, but the youth pastor was out of order in the way he handled the situation. Because I'm their boss, my will has to be done in the situation, and they had the choice to come into order and honor my will—or not.

The young man had had the opportunity to use his gifts and growing influence, but by not serving well and by being out of order, he obstructed promotion. The youth pastor had the chance to use honor to bring his assistant back into order, but by not addressing the issue in an orderly manner, he had sown disorder.

Atmosphere Produces Change

Honoring God's will on earth can be challenging, especially when people appointed over us make it difficult. A young woman who volunteered with us felt called to work with our ministry, but her parents wanted her to move back to Malaysia. What did she do? Did she tell them off because she had a higher calling than obeying her parents? That would have been out of order. Instead, I watched this young woman's influence increase as she prayed that God would change her parents' hearts. Because of her attitude, she gained credibility and influence with her parents—and with me. So much so that we gave her a position on staff, and her ability grew and grew until she became a regional pastor as well as our CFO. Her credibility and influence created an atmosphere of promotion.

> *IF OUR INFLUENCE IS BAD, THE ATMOSPHERE WE CREATE WILL BE BAD. BUT IF OUR INFLUENCE IS GOOD AND GODLY, IT WILL PRODUCE A KINGDOM ATMOSPHERE.*

If our influence is bad, the atmosphere we create will be bad. But if our influence is good and godly, it will produce a kingdom atmosphere.

Which atmosphere are we called to create? Our Father's. At our church, we tell staff members they are to create the atmosphere that Sam and I are creating under God's direction. Anything other than that is out of order and would be a clash of atmospheres. That's why honor and order are such big deals.

Atmospheres, then, produce change. We hear from God a lot at Planetshakers Awakenings—the atmosphere is amazing, and the presence of God is incredible. Why? Because we use gifts to serve the body of Christ, we have gained credibility and influence, and that has created an atmosphere of worship. That atmosphere allows us to produce change.

But it doesn't stop there. Changes for the good produce seed. In God's presence, He will seed you with

> *WHERE THERE IS NO ORDER, EVEN HONOR CANNOT PRODUCE FRUITFULNESS.*

greatness. Do you think if you were in the presence of some of the most successful people on earth that some of their thinking and "greatness" might rub off on you? That by being in their presence you might pick up a thing or two? What would make us think any less of spending time with God?

When we're out on our own and don't operate under proper authority from the head, we can't receive the anointing that starts from the head and flows down. We won't bear fruit if we don't receive seed. And fruit produces dominion.

Honor + Order = Fruitfulness

Where there is no order, even honor cannot produce fruitfulness. Both honor and order must be present for our lives to be as fruitful and satisfying as God intends for them to be. If you want to be a person of order and fruitfulness, it begins with the goal to reflect the Father through your life. Jesus did what He saw the Father doing, and we in turn do what we see

Jesus do. We do what He instructs us to do in His Word and in the individual words and corporate words we receive. When we release our gifts, through honor, as long as it is in this system of order, it represents what heaven is like and will follow the process of fruitfulness.

I love it when my children represent me. Recently, I saw my son, Jonathan, from a distance, lifting his hands and jumping during worship. When I saw him praising and worshiping God, I was extremely blessed. I don't want my son to perform for a crowd; I want him to encounter God.

While Jonathan is like me, my daughter, Aimee, is like my wife, Sam. She's a mini Sam. My children have their own expressions and worship, but they also represent their mother and father. However, when there are things that don't look good on them, it's our job to help them reflect Jesus.

Jesus, whose purpose on this earth was to represent the Father, was both God and man. In the Garden of Gethsemane, He displayed His humanity as He struggled with what was to come on the cross. "My Father," He prayed, "if it is possible, may this cup be taken from me" (Matthew 26:39). Right here, we see that even the Son of God had to submit willingly to God's order. And the Father had to hold Him to it.

As a parent, sometimes we try to fix circumstances for our children instead of bringing them into order. I've done that both as a father and a leader. But instead of fixing the situation, God often desires to fix His *children*.

The real blessing comes when the children are in order. We read the end of what Jesus said in the quote above to find the right attitude: "Yet not as I will, but as you will."

What would have happened if the Father had been sympathetic with Jesus in the garden and, instead of sending Him to the cross, had done something to violate His own order? What if God had let Jesus off the hook? All of humanity would have suffered for it—eternally.

We often want to please people, but pleasing isn't bringing people or things into order. When we love people we bring them into order.

The Vine

God loves us so much, He is willing to bring us into order even when it means pruning us. In John 15, Jesus says, "I am the true vine, and my Father is the gardener. He cuts off every branch in me that bears no fruit, while every branch that does bear fruit he prunes so that it will be even more fruitful" (John 15:1–2).

For those reading this who are not into gardening, pruning is a process of cutting away branches and shoots on a vine for a purpose. It isn't done to destroy the plant; it's a strategic cutting that causes a plant to bear even more fruit.

Jesus goes on to say, "You have already been pruned and purified by the message I have given you. Remain in me, and I will remain in you. For a branch cannot produce fruit if it is severed from the vine, and you cannot be fruitful unless you remain in me" (John 15:3–4 NLT). He is the vine, and we are the branches, and when we remain in Him

> GOD LOVES US SO MUCH, HE IS WILLING TO BRING US INTO ORDER EVEN WHEN IT MEANS PRUNING US.

(remember walking with the Dove in mind?) we produce much fruit. "For apart from Me," Jesus says, "you can do nothing" (John 15:5 NLT).

What about those who don't honor, those who refuse to be in order? Jesus tells us that those people—who have severed themselves—will be thrown away like a useless branch, where they'll wither.

But here comes the promise: "But if you remain in me and my words remain in you, you may ask for anything you want, and it will be granted! When you produce much fruit, you are my true disciples. This brings great glory to my Father" (John 15:7–8 NLT).

Why does God want us to produce much fruit? Because that's how we subdue nations and expand the dominion of the kingdom of God. That's how we bring great glory to the Father.

Come Back

Perhaps you're reading this and you think that because you've messed up in life you're a branch that has been tossed away to wither. Does that mean you're out of order for life? No, and that's the great thing about God's message to us: His grace. If God waited until we were in order before He offered salvation, none of us would be saved. If God waited for us to fix ourselves, none of us could recover from a sin or a fall.

If there is one concept I wish for you to grasp in this book it is the image of the honoring father from the story of the prodigal son. What did he do with the son who was out of order? He brought him back in grace, covered his disorder, and restored him. God's kindness leads us to repentance, not His judgment (Romans 2:4). The order of the kingdom is kindness, goodness, and grace.

But the truth remains: You won't receive God's commanded blessing if you're out of order.

I've watched people who were close to me slip out of order and move away from the Vine and from what God called Sam and I to do with our ministry. We prayed for them and asked God to change their hearts; we did everything we could, but some refused to accept God's order.

IF GOD WAITED FOR US TO FIX OURSELVES, NONE OF US COULD RECOVER FROM A SIN OR A FALL.

I don't believe they lost their salvation—they're still in God's family. But they're not producing fruit. And I can only imagine the pain God feels, for the pain I've felt when these people cut themselves away from fruitfulness was profound. People always look at the pain of the person who is severed, but I believe it is far more painful for the Father who produced them.

Some people feel that God's order is restrictive and controlling, but He's no more controlling than a seatbelt or the rules for safe driving on the road. If you're out of order when you drive your car, you can hurt and kill people.

Order isn't control. It's protection.

The heart of the Father is for every one of His children to be in order and to be part of His kingdom. If you're out of order, His desire isn't to make you suffer; it's to draw you in. He wants you to receive the full extent of His blessings and to experience great fruitfulness. You can only do this when you are in order.

CHAPTER 15

HIGHER AUTHORITY

nce, when I was a young youth leader and pastor's kid, a pastor invited me to speak in Singapore. I was extremely new to the ministry, and the pastor who invited me made a huge impact on my understanding of honor. The way he honored me and looked after a twenty-six-year-old speaker who was still wet behind the ears showed me how to treat other people and other ministries. He rolled out the red carpet and treated me with a first-class attitude and spirit of excellence. It helped form who I am today.

But the way he treated me didn't just influence how I view honoring guest speakers, it also opened my eyes to a new understanding of authority: You can't impart what you don't possess.

God has built something into the power of honor that enables people in leadership to honor the gifts in others and bring them out in a powerful way. You can honor a friend or a peer, and you can honor leaders over you, but there's something dynamic about receiving honor from an authority. People in positions of authority can honor us and bring our gifts out of us in ways that make a great impact on the lives of others.

As a young man fresh in ministry, I began to benefit from the authority on other ministries. Instead of trying to compete with them, I honored them, and some amazing leaders honored me as well. People like Bill Johnson had a significant impact on my ministry—not because he took me under his wing or mentored me, but because the authority he conveyed brought out my gifts and shaped my ministry as I read his books.

I would love to say that I benefited from the direct authority of pastors like Bishop T. D. Jakes and his breakthrough anointing. Again, however, I benefited from honoring his messages long before I ever met him. By honoring these men and others, I released inheritance, and their authority conveyed what they possessed in an amazing way.

Authority Must Back It Up

In the previous chapter I said that your gift will create influence and credibility in your life. You gain credibility through what God's gift allows you to do—and how you do it. Your dominion in an area is what produces authority.

If you have authority to back up what you say, when you add honor you get a total bigger than the sum of your parts— you get multiplication.

I can remember when our church honored Robert Morris and his teaching on the blessed life. When you look at the fruit in his own life, you can see the man has authority to speak on giving and finances. Multiple times, he has literally given away everything because God told him to—cars, houses, life savings. There's an authority behind what he says. When he delivers a word from God on giving Him your first and best, Robert's word carries authority.

When people in our church heard his message and honored him by responding, the results were nothing short of amazing. We didn't experience addition; we experienced *multiplication*. We saw jobs, financial increase, divine provision, and increased faithfulness and giving throughout the congregation.

I would never invite someone to my church to release an anointing for business and to be the next Donald Trump who was an unemployed bum off the street. He wouldn't have the authority behind anything he said. Even if he knew all the right words, he would lack the authority.

Glen Berteau, who shared that message "Devil, Your Request Has Been Denied," spoke at a Planetshakers conference when we were still new. He said to me, "People don't praise and worship that much anymore, and the Spirit of worship here is amazing. You guys are really into praise and worship. I could've cooked, you're so hungry for God!

"But when it comes to the Word, you're dead. There's no life. You just sit there and listen, but there's no response."

I nodded and said, "Oh, okay."

But he shook his head and said, "No."

My acknowledgment wasn't enough. Then he began to impart the authority that he carried into my ministry. His congregation responds to the Word, and he had the authority to convey that anointing. In the middle of his speaking, our conference exploded into praise for nearly half an hour—about the Word of God! It was a supernatural praise without the band, and it shook the rafters at 122 decibels!

> HONOR CREATES A GREAT ATMOSPHERE WHERE ANYTHING CAN HAPPEN.

We actually recorded it, but the people were so loud that he couldn't finish his sermon because God had moved and exploded in that place. That never would have happened if he hadn't had that authority on his life. Glen brought an impartation, but we honored it—and it has stayed with us since! Now when folks come to our church they see that the people not only worship, they respond to the Word.

Double Portion

Recall from the story of Elijah and Elisha mentioned in a previous chapter that Elisha wanted a double portion of the anointing that was on his master, and he received it. He asked for a hard thing, but he honored his teacher at the close of his ministry just as he had honored him for the years they were together.

Elisha couldn't have received a double portion had Elijah not had the authority to impart it. Now, that was two generations. Imagine what would have happened if someone had honored the anointing on Elisha's life as he had honored that which was upon Elijah. We would know that prophet's name and all of his deeds, and I believe he wouldn't have received a double portion but a multiplied inheritance and anointing.

Honor creates a great atmosphere where anything can happen. People grow in an atmosphere of honor, but what brings true momentum is honor *and* authority.

You could honor me for an inheritance of a million dollars, but since I don't have a million to give you, you wouldn't see a cent of it, let alone a double portion!

When you honor someone whose gift is in its infancy, you can help release and nurture that gift. When you honor someone whose gift is mature, you invite strength, authority, and multiplication into your life.

If you want true multiplication, you must honor someone who carries the authority in an area—this will grow your gift exponentially. When you honor people who carry authority along with the gifts God has placed in their lives, He can create multiplication in your life.

God Multiplies Planetshakers

When we first started a Planetshakers conference, God didn't really begin to multiply it until our second year. A guest speaker named Rich Wilkerson spoke that year. Rich ran a youth conference and had been a youth evangelist. He had an authority on his life for ministering to young people.

That year he shared a message called "I Want the Cross"— basically a cry for young people to lay their lives down for the cause of Jesus. It's his life message, and he himself had lived it, laying his own life down for the cross. He spoke with authentic authority, and our people honored his message. It actually shifted the atmosphere of Planetshakers, and we haven't been the same since.

It's hard to describe exactly what happened, but the atmosphere shifted from a general desire to empower young people to the specific call to lay down our lives for the cause of Christ. Rich's authority was far greater than our experience was at that time, and it multiplied the momentum of our conference. We shared his message all over Australia, and for the next conference we had buses full of kids driving forty-eight hours from faraway towns to attend.

We had 300 kids our first year, but we had 700 for our day service and 1,200 at night that second year. People began to say that God was moving at Planetshakers, and I believe the change occurred because the authority that was on Rich Wilkerson's life released multiplication.

God has brought many different ministries into our lives to impact the people attending Planetshakers Awakenings and to our church in Australia. I mentioned how lives were changed in our church when Robert Morris shared the concept that we give to give, not to get back. I had already known and taught that we give to build the kingdom, but the authority he carried on his life changed the atmosphere. Giving in our church went up 75 percent that

HONOR RELEASES INHERITANCE, BUT HONOR PLUS AUTHORITY YIELDS MULTIPLICATION.

year and has stayed there, because people honored the word Robert Morris brought.

Honor releases inheritance, but honor plus authority yields multiplication. When you sincerely want to grow something in your life for God, He will pour blessings upon you as you receive from people and ministries who have a greater anointing than you have in a particular area. As you honor that anointing, it will multiply.

Dead Bones Can Live

What did Elisha do to receive his double portion? He honored what was on Elijah. The sad thing is that no one apparently honored what was on Elisha. God wanted to do it. This is evident from an event that took place after Elisha's death. When some Israelites were burying a man, they spied a band of raiders coming their way. They hastily threw the corpse into Elisha's tomb and fled. The Bible tells us, "When the body touched Elisha's bones, the man came to life and stood up on his feet" (2 Kings 13:21). Even after that amazing experience, no one took up Elisha's mantle—and no one experienced an inheritance of multiplication.

Joshua honored the promise that was on Moses. When Moses went up the mountain, Joshua wasn't down with the people and Aaron making a golden calf; he was halfway up the mountain waiting eagerly for Moses.

Joshua was one of the spies who entered the Promised Land, and he and Caleb were the ones who said, "Yes, the enemy is big, but our God is bigger!" Unfortunately, they were overruled by their faithless colleagues, and through no fault of his own, Joshua had to wander the wilderness with the rest of God's people.

While in the wilderness, he had a choice: let the wilderness get in him, or keep living for the promise. He didn't face that choice for a day or a week—he faced the challenge and refused to agree with the lie of the wilderness for *forty years*. He never let the wilderness get in him; he kept living the promise.

IF YOU HONOR THE TRUTH, THE CONDITIONS OF LIFE WILL BOW TO THE POSITION OF TRUTH.

Joshua understood the power of honoring the authority on Moses, and it wasn't Moses who led the children of Israel into the Promised Land but Joshua. Joshua became a powerful leader after he cut his teeth by trusting God to bring down Jericho's walls. The sun actually stood still because Joshua prayed, and while it shone, the Israelites routed their enemies. Joshua continued to honor what God had said He would do, and because of that, he took his Promised Land. If you honor the truth, the conditions of life will bow to the position of truth.

But again, though Joshua inherited great authority, the generation that followed didn't honor what Joshua had. That authority faltered with the third generation.

What would have happened if someone had followed in Joshua's steps as he had followed in Moses' steps? Would there still have been pagan people in the land, or would Israel have had a united kingdom long before Saul and David?

Fruit

It's all well and good for me to talk about receiving from the anointing on ministries such as T. D. Jakes', Robert Morris', and others. You may think that you don't roll with that crowd. First, let me remind you that long before major ministries came to speak at Planetshakers Awakenings or at our church, I honored the anointing on their lives and ministries by listening to their messages and reading their books.

But let me bring this to a more practical level. There's something dynamic about receiving personally from someone with authority. So how do you do that? And how do you know someone has authority?

Remember what I've said about intimacy—your life will look like what you are intimate with. You will know whose lives you want to emulate when you see the fruit of their lives.

How do you know people have authority? They have the fruit to prove it.

As you adopt a lifestyle of honor, you'll want to take that to the next level by honoring those who have authority in an area. Honor them for the gifts God has put in their lives, and look for the credibility, character, and fruit that come with a life of honor.

When you're kingdom-minded, you can expect the byproduct of honoring authority to create a multiplied outcome. But the principle

> *YOU WILL KNOW WHOSE LIVES YOU WANT TO EMULATE WHEN YOU SEE THE FRUIT OF THEIR LIVES.*

is the same whether or not the authority is of God's kingdom, and you can use this principle in various walks of life. If you honor the authority on the successful businessman's life, it can bring multiplication into your life. If you honor the authority on the life of an amazing wife and mother, it can bring multiplication into your life.

Just be careful whom you honor.

It's vital that you are intentional about honoring the authority on a person's life but equally important that you are intentional in selecting whose authority you honor. Keep in mind what I said about chicken bones—to an extent you can take the good and leave the bad. However, Jesus tells us that a tree is known by its fruit—a good tree doesn't bear bad fruit, and a bad tree doesn't bear good fruit (Luke 6:43).

Look at the fruit in people's lives and honor their gifts, then praise and thank God for the authority He has put on their lives and the power that honor has to release that into your life.

Do you feel like there is no one who will draw out your gift? Do you feel like you have a small, underdeveloped gift because there is no one to mentor you, to believe in you? Take heart, for there's hope. God has not left you helpless. If you don't have someone who believes in you, know that *God* believes in you, and He can provide people who bear great authority to draw out your gift—even across long distances. You can be mentored from a distance, even from people you have never met. Study and invest yourself in the words they share. Look for the fruit of their authority, honor it no matter where you are, and trust God to bring the inheritance—and the multiplication.

Do you want to take your gift further? Honor is the key. Honor people with authority, even from a distance, and honor those around you who need their gifts brought out. Have a heaven mindset, check your motives—that you are not honoring just to receive but because it is part of God's order—and expect His commanded blessing as you come into unity with parts of the body of Christ that may not be close geographically but are your family in the kingdom of God.

Does distance mean anything to the Lord? Do you think that a generational inheritance is limited by geography? Your honor creates an environment of growth for the gift God has placed in your life, and authority gives it legs—propels it forward.

Do you want your family to be blessed? Do you want your business to multiply? Do you want to see your city won for Christ? Well, this is how you do it. You'll be amazed what God will do in your life when you honor the gift and God in those around you, particularly those with authority. Get ready for multiplication!

CHAPTER 16

HONOR THE TRUTH

Growing up the son of a pastor, ministry was part of my life. I was in church at least three times a week— even before I was born! I grew up in a good home with parents who believed in me. In fact, they encouraged me to discover what I was called to do; they didn't expect me to follow in their footsteps and didn't pressure me to do that.

Even so, I grew up with doubts and insecurities. I remember encountering Jesus as a kid, and while it was awesome, at the same time I started to believe some lies about myself and to come into agreement with my insecurities.

We have a choice every day whether to agree with what God says about us and honor that, or to honor what our situation says—and what the devil says. Did you know that you can be in conversation with the devil and not even realize it? When that insidious voice of doubt and fear creeps into the back of your mind, you can be sure it's a conversation with your enemy and what he says, not what God says.

The Bible tells us that the devil is under our feet, so why is he so often in our heads? The devil only gets in our heads when we come down to his level. We can allow him to speak into our heads—when we should be standing on his head!

It's no accident that the thing God calls you to do is the thing the devil attacks. Is God's promise to you under assault right now? That proves it's a promise to cling to!

"I Can't Be a Preacher"

I remember my mom telling me so often how special I was and that God had a plan for my life. As I mentioned previously, I often received prophecies about what God was going to do with my life. This should have encouraged me and given me great confidence, but instead it discouraged me. I didn't want to be a preacher because I thought I couldn't be as good a preacher as my dad was. I reminded myself again and again that I couldn't do it like my dad did it, like my grandfather did it , or my cousin, or my brother did it.

> IT'S NO ACCIDENT THAT THE THING GOD CALLS YOU TO DO IS THE THING THE DEVIL ATTACKS.

I loved music, and before I was called, I didn't want to be a preacher—I wanted to be a rock star! Music didn't trigger any of the insecurities I harbored about what God was calling me to do.

I shared with you how at age fifteen I received a word that I would be a spokesman to the nations. Instead of feeling good about that, I was cynical. Some older women in our church came up to me after I received that word and said, "You're going to be just like your dad." Being a cheeky little guy, I said back to them, "What? Short and fat?"

God wanted to free me from the urge to compare myself to my father and the other preachers in our family through that word. Though God spoke to me, I couldn't process it because I was so insecure. My heart was a negative filter for what I had received. Because I harbored lies and insecurities in my heart, it filtered what I heard and created mounting pressure. *You can't do it. You can't even communicate—and you'll never be as good as your dad or your grandfather,"* a voice told me.

The problem was, I agreed with that voice.

Oh, I had reasons to feel insecure, and I clearly remember where some of these lies got started or were reinforced. The band I played with, More Than Conquerors, did a show, and I had to introduce one song. I was fifteen and a bit of a late bloomer, so my voice was changing. I got up to introduce the song, and as I said, "If you don't know Jesus, you really need Him," my voice cracked on "need." A couple of people smiled a bit, but I just went on and played the song.

Afterwards, we watched the video. When we came to the point where I said, "You really need Him," everyone laughed, including me. But then they rewound it and played it over and over again. They didn't play it a few times, they played it fifty times! Though I laughed on the outside, on the inside I made agreement with a lie: *I will never speak in public again!*

I was bound by this lie and others like it for years.

When I told you about my English teacher, I didn't mention that while she probably didn't like me very much, she was perhaps trying to handle me as she had my brother. When people challenged my brother, he answered right back and tried to prove them wrong. While I was good at math, and sports, and history, I was only okay at English. And I certainly wasn't my brother—instead of seeking to prove a person wrong, I responded to a challenge by saying, "Yeah, you're right." So instead of rising to the English teacher's challenge, I wilted under her criticism and a report that pointedly said I couldn't communicate.

I agreed with the lies that I couldn't match up to what this or that person had done and I compared myself to them. I agreed with a lie when I made a fool of myself introducing that song, and it was reinforced when my English teacher said I couldn't communicate. These and many other lies formed the foundation of my insecurity.

NEVER AGREE WITH THE LIE THAT YOU ARE DEFEATED.

And I came into agreement with them. I honored the lies, and the lies dictated how I lived my life—up until I had an encounter with God at youth camp. When I told Jesus I couldn't communicate, things changed as He declared a word over me. He told me, "Yes you can. Here is My power."

Instead of agreeing with the lies about my life, I came into agreement with God's truth about my life. I finally honored what God said about me and not what the enemy said about me.

Get Back on the Bike

Have you ever listened to what the devil has said about you instead of what God has said about you? Have you ever let your circumstance dictate what you think is true—even if God has told you something else? Maybe you've tried to do something and it didn't work the first time, so you thought, *"Well, that isn't for me."*

What would have happened if you had responded to that experience like a person learning to ride a bike? If you decided you were incapable of riding a bike the first time you fell and hurt your knee, you never would have ridden a bike. To think we can't do something just because it's hard is as foolish as thinking we'll never be able to ride a bike just because we fall off once or twice. Instead of coming into agreement with lies, we must get up and dare to ride again. If you fall off, get back on and ride—as many times as it takes!

Never agree with the lie that you are defeated. You are more than a conqueror through Jesus Christ, and when you honor His words about you, you buy into the idea that He can do anything through you. When you refuse to buy into lies, you can face disappointment or rejection firm in the knowledge of who you are in Christ. Then, if healing doesn't come when you want it, or financial trouble seems to keep getting worse, or the breakthrough you're believing for doesn't happen in your timing, you won't buy into the lie but will stay firm.

Rejected

I told you about the time I bought a t-shirt for a woman's husband who was dying of cancer. But that's not the first time the Lord has encouraged me to do something like that. Once I was at a gas station and the woman in front of me had left her money at home. The Holy Spirit spoke to me and said, "Pay for her gas." I was embarrassed, but I said, "Excuse me, but I'll pay for your gas."

The lady said, "Pardon?" I told her that I would pay for it, and she said, "No, you can't do that." I insisted, and I handed the clerk my card. The woman gushed and said, "Thank you so much!"

I told her to have a blessed day, and when I stepped up to the clerk to pay for my own gas, he said, "What was that?" I explained that I felt like God had told me to do it. I could tell it made an impression on him.

I was in another gas station when something similar happened. This time a gentleman had forgotten his money, and once again I felt the Lord impress me to pay for his gas. I volunteered, but the man said, "No, you can't do that." I smiled and told him it was okay, but he refused. He wouldn't let me pay.

After my previous amazing experience, I was disappointed. "God, I thought you told me to do that," I complained. I now had a choice: The next time God told me to do something like that, would I do it? Would I let my disappointment override my desire to honor and obey Him?

You can either live conditionally or positionally. You can live according to what God says and honor that, or you can live according to what your circumstances, the devil, or your insecurities say. What will you do when you're rejected? What will you do when things are hard? Will you continue to honor God, or will you honor what the enemy brings into your life?

Even after God called me to be a minister and said that I would be a spokesman to the world, and I

> YOU CAN LIVE ACCORDING TO WHAT GOD SAYS AND HONOR THAT, OR YOU CAN LIVE ACCORDING TO WHAT YOUR CIRCUMSTANCES, THE DEVIL, OR YOUR INSECURITIES SAY.

agreed with it, I continued to battle insecurity. The first time I ministered at a youth camp, I was prayed up and had practiced in front of the mirror a great deal. I was as prepared as I could be—and it was good!

There were perhaps 150 kids in attendance, and I preached what I thought was a stirring message and gave an altar call. No one moved. I kept speaking, determined to get someone to move. I think the kids began to get hungry, and finally someone took one for the team—I think he stood up because he thought if someone didn't go forward, I would go on and on for the rest of the day.

I went back to my room and said, *"God, you have the wrong person again."* God told me something I'll never forget: "No, I have the right person. You just need to get out of the way!" I asked what He meant, and He told me, "You're trying too hard, and that's stopping what I want to do."

The next session, I didn't feel like I preached well. But when I said, "God wants to touch you, why don't you come forward?"

The whole place came up to the front! It was unbelievable! As I watched all these young people come forward, God said, "See, when you work with Me, you win. When you're worried about impressing people, you are buying into a lie."

This was how I began to honor God in ministry.

At times God has told me to do something and I've complained that I didn't want to because I felt I would look silly. That insecurity was the voice of the enemy trying to keep me from honoring the Lord. When we face situations like this, we have a choice: Will we honor a lie, or will we honor what God says? When I choose to honor God, I'm always blessed—even if not in the way I expect.

Do you know what it takes to be victorious in this life? Get up just one more time than you fall down! Get back on the bike, learn to ride, and work with God to win!

An All-Access Pass

We have a choice every day to believe what God says and to honor that, or to honor our circumstances and what the devil says. God says we are joint heirs with Christ. Do you believe that?

First, what is an heir? It's someone who inherits. Notice, I didn't say it's someone who is going to inherit. We don't have to wait for someone to die before we inherit; we inherit *daily*. My children are my heirs. Yes, they will inherit something when I die, but they also inherit things today. They receive their inheritance by living in my house and by experiencing my blessing and provision.

We travel all over the world to do Planetshakers Awakenings, and we typically hire big stadiums for the events. You need passes to get into certain areas, and because my children are my heirs, they get all-access passes and can go anywhere they like. I remember a time when a large security guard stopped my son at the door. I was inside and could only see this from a distance, but when this giant man said "You can't go in there!" my son said, "Yes I can, here's my pass." The guard questioned where he got it, and my son confidently replied, "From my dad. He's the boss!"

WHEN I CHOOSE TO HONOR GOD, I'M ALWAYS BLESSED—EVEN IF NOT IN THE WAY I EXPECT.

We can boldly approach our Father because we have an all-access pass—the blood of Jesus Christ, spilled for the redemption of many. When we honor that and receive His free gift, we're not only adopted and made sons and daughters of God, we wear His blood like a badge. It's an all-access pass to the throne room of grace, into the very presence of God!

As His children, we receive inheritance daily. When my son was little, he learned to roll down the windows in our car by pressing the button—which he did once in the car wash! One time I was about to go into a gas station to pay when he rolled down the window and asked, "Dad, can I have a lollipop?" He was very little, and though I said, "Sure, no problem," he continued to ask repeatedly. He was asking for an inheritance as my heir, but because he was so young he didn't understand I had already agreed to his request. He asked and kept on asking—even when I had already gone inside the gas station. He unbuckled himself

WE DON'T NEED TO BEG; AS SONS AND DAUGHTERS WE HAVE ONLY TO ASK.

and entered the shop and asked again, "May I have a lollipop?"

As easy as it was for me to buy a lollipop for my son, your Father is rich enough to give you any blessing you ask Him for in the name of His Son. The Bible tells us to ask and keep on asking, to knock and keep on knocking—but not because we must pester God into blessing us. We must ask and keep on asking because there will be times that don't work out as we expect, and we will face a daily choice of whether to honor and agree with God's promises or to be in agreement with a lie.

We don't need to beg; as sons and daughters we have only to ask. It's easier for God to meet your need for healing, breakthrough, provision, peace, joy, and so much more than it was for me to buy my son a lollipop. But when you don't understand the circumstances in your life and you think God hasn't come through for you, will you still have faith and honor?

The devil says that God doesn't care about you, that He doesn't want to bless you or heal you. He uses the same lies he's been using since the beginning: that God isn't quite as good as He says He is. You have a choice of whether to believe this or not. Who is the liar? The devil, or God and His Word?

Mighty in Words and Powerful in Deeds

It's tempting to think that the stories in the Bible are about people who were different from us. It's easy to think that they didn't have any trouble trusting God because their circumstances were different, or because their backgrounds were different. Do they ever seem like superheroes to you? Children's books about the Bible make them seem like that, but nothing could be further from the truth. They were as full of frailties, insecurities, and lies as anyone else.

So how did they become the heroes of the Bible? They honored.

Think of Moses, who encountered a bush on fire that didn't burn and heard the voice of I Am. His past had so colored his view of himself that Moses argued with God when God told him to go back to Pharoah and demand the release of God's people. He was so in agreement with the lie that he couldn't speak that Moses fought God on every point.

The thing is, at one point Moses was a prince in Pharaoh's house, and the Bible describes him as being mighty in word and powerful in

> **BUT GOD IS GRACIOUS, AND HE WORKS THROUGH OUR WEAKNESSES.**

deed. When did he begin to stutter? When did he start to have problems with his words? I believe that when he fled Egypt he bought into a lie—and it changed his words.

In the burning bush conversation, God showed Moses miracle after miracle, but still Moses doubted. He clung to his lies.

But God is gracious, and He works through our weaknesses. God still used Moses and allowed Aaron, Moses' brother, to go with him and speak for him. God did many mighty miracles through Moses, and the very foundation of our Judeo-Christian faith was formed by his words.

Then came the day when God told him to speak to a rock. God had allowed Moses a season of grace, had allowed him to make choices to believe and to reject the lies. God had showed Moses how good He is, and then God gave him a chance to deal with the thing that had been holding him back.

But instead of speaking to the rock, this greatly revered man—writer of the Torah and one of the greatest figures in the Jewish faith—struck it instead. God didn't let Moses enter the Promised Land, but this wasn't simply because he hit a rock. In some ways, Moses had never completely rejected the lies. He had never completely bought into what God had said he was capable of.

This lack of honor kept him from the Promised Land.

Have lies turned you from a person mighty of word and deed into a frightened stutterer? What lies are you believing that might keep you from what God has promised?

The Umpire

I am a big tennis fan, and when I was younger I was actually pretty good at the game. If you've watched the game of tennis like I have, you know about the lines people. Their job is to determine whether the ball is in or out. The problem is that anytime they speak up it's always negative. They never call the ball "in"; the only time they say anything it's, "Out!"

Life is like the game of tennis, and the devil has set himself up as the linesman. He's waiting to call your dream, your promise, your future, and your blessing "Out!" The problem is, if you don't rise to the challenge, you can agree with his call and just wait for the next set. You can agree with him.

Some players are quiet and passive, but you may remember John McEnroe, a brilliant tennis player. He must have thought he had the best sight in the world, because he could be flat on his back on the tennis court and still see better than anyone else—especially the lines people! They would call it out, and he would argue with them incessantly. He was not going to let anyone rob him of his victory.

Now, I don't suggest you use the same language he did. But when the devil calls your dream out, as a son or daughter of God, it's your job to stand your ground and say, "No!" Tell him *no* when he says your family is out, your job is out, your health is out, or your dream is out. You have a choice to stand your ground, to believe a lie or honor truth.

When we stand our ground but appear to be in a stalemate, we must look high above the court of life to the Umpire. He is seated high above this world, enthroned with every power. He is high and lifted up, and you can appeal to Him. He's the one in charge, and when you know His Word, you can stand your ground based on His rulebook of life. You can say, "The linesman says it's out, but this Book says it's in. Which is it?"

So God gets out the rulebook to show the linesman what the Word says. He shows the linesman that you are created in God's image and that He has blessed you to be fruitful and multiply. It says God's plans for you are good, to prosper you and not to harm you. It says no weapon formed against you will prosper. It says you are more than a conqueror. It says greater is

He who is in you than he who is in the world. It says you can do all things through Christ who gives you strength.

God shows the linesmen all of these things, and then He gets to the end where the contract for the new covenant is signed. It's red—blood red. The title says King of kings, Lord of lords, Lion of the tribe of Judah, Prince of Peace. Written in His own blood it says *JESUS.*

Then the Umpire makes His decision:

"Overruled."

With His finger pointing at the devil, God says, "Your ruling on this life is overruled! I call it 'in,' not 'out.'"

Do you feel that the devil has called your health out? Your dream out? Your family out? You have a choice—whose report will you believe? Whose words will you honor?

Seated or Defeated

We learned at the beginning of this book that honor means to esteem at the highest degree and give weight to. Whose words carry the most weight with you, God's words or the devil's?

What lies are you believing today?

I believe there's an anointing right now as you read this for the Holy Spirit to reveal the lies that are holding you back. I've experienced God's breakthrough in this area, and I believe He has given me authority to speak on honor and freedom. If something has dogged your steps, held you back, kept you bound, and brought you pain, I want you to pray with me and let go of the lies.

Dear Jesus, I'm sorry for believing a lie. I choose to honor You and what You say. Change my heart to honor Your truth and what You have said about me—that I am an heir of God, and I am adopted into His family. Show me any lie that is holding me back, and bring your truth to overcome every device of the enemy. Thank you for setting me free!

I urge you to read through Romans eight, because it explains your position in Christ so well. Ephesians 2:6 says that you are seated in heavenly places, so you have the choice of whether to believe a lie or the truth—to live seated or defeated.

I once spoke at a meeting when the Lord told me that there was a twelve-year-old girl with a broken leg in attendance and that God wanted to heal her. Now, I'd like to say I immediately trusted God and His word to me, but I'm not that spiritual. I intentionally dropped a pen on the floor and looked under the chairs—I didn't see any casts. I complained to the Lord that there was no one there with a broken leg, but He said there was.

How do you know? I asked.

"I'm God."

Good point. He told me to give an invitation for healing, but I kept arguing in my spirit. I worried what would happen if I gave that invitation and no one came forward or was healed. I thought they would quit listening to me. I worried that if it didn't work, I would get the blame—but if it did happen, God would get the glory. How is that fair, I wondered?

I got up and had everyone close their eyes—I didn't want them to see me. I then said that a twelve-year-old girl with a broken leg was there and that God wanted to heal her. Suddenly in the back corner, a hand went up. A girl I had not seen all meeting gathered her crutches and came up to me. I didn't feel any great power, but I felt good that God had come through. In fact, I preached so well that morning I bought my own CD! God healed that girl, and He taught me a great lesson about choosing to trust Him.

I had a choice of whether to live defeated or to be seated with God. I had a choice whether to live for a lie based on my own insecurities and worries about what people would think, or to honor the word He had declared over me and believe that I am an heir of God.

Chosen

Do you know that God had to make a choice about you?

Before we became pregnant, my wife and I believed for a long time that God would give us children. But we just couldn't get pregnant. After five years, a prophet, who didn't know about our situation, told my mother-in-law that we would be pregnant within six months. We stood firm on that word—and were pregnant in just three!

Now, we did have some complications, but God was with us. Since it was our first baby, we didn't know what to expect. After twenty-five hours of trying to deliver our son, the doctor decided that my wife needed a C-section.

I put on a little blue suit, and we went into another room so they could operate on Sam. They asked me if I wanted to watch them pull out the baby, but I said, "No, thank you. I'll just minister to my wife right here. *She* needs me." Of course, if I had gone on the other side of the curtain, I would have fallen down—and it wouldn't have been under the power of God!

The doctors delivered a healthy baby boy. Since my family predominantly has boys, when they asked if I wanted to look at the sex of the baby, I was confident. "Evans have boys." My grandfather was a boy, my father was a boy, and I'm a boy. My mother? She was there to have boys!

> GOD HAD A CHOICE, AND HE CHOSE YOU!

So we had a beautiful baby boy, and when we got pregnant again, we didn't check the sex of the baby before birth. I thought, "Well, it's probably a boy. The Evans family has boys."

This time we booked the C-section at 8:00 a.m. The baby was out by 8:15 a.m., and I was on the golf course by 9:00 a.m.! No, just joking.

This time they reached in and pulled out . . . a healthy baby girl! "You have a girl," they told me. "A girl?" I asked. Evans have boys . . . I never understood how amazing girls can be! My family only knew boys, and I'm so happy I have an amazing daughter, Aimee.

I tell you this to make a final point. We couldn't choose whether we had a boy or girl. We couldn't pick eye color, hair color, or personality. We couldn't choose their gifts.

You may never have thought this about God, but He adopted you—He picked you. He chose you. God had a choice, and He chose you!

Now *you* have a choice. When the devil says that you're no good, you're hopeless, and that nothing good will ever happen in your life, you have a choice—will you honor the lie or will you honor God's love?

You can believe that you're an heir of God, chosen before the foundation of the world. You can choose to believe that you're adopted, chosen, bought with a price. You can believe that God loves you so much He was willing to do whatever it took to get you. It cost Him Jesus, who died to pay for your life with His blood.

You get to choose what you honor, and, when you buy into the generational inheritance that God has purposed for your life, you reciprocate the honor He extended to you from the beginning. Honor began with Him, and like the honoring father of the prodigal story, God has never stopped looking for you and waiting to honor you.

When you reciprocate the honor our Father extends to you, it unlocks the same power that raised Christ from the dead into your life. Honor is the key to unlock a limitless life. Choose honor, and live seated next to Christ. Bring heaven down to earth so that all the blessings of God may be commanded into your life.

It's time to release your inheritance. It's time to choose honor and use the key God has provided for you.

EPILOGUE

t's an exciting journey, this journey of honor. It's vulnerable. It's releasing. When we truly understand honor and the power of honor to release heaven on earth, this takes away the crutches we've hobbled on. The healing, breakthrough, blessing, and generational inheritance that honor releases from God takes us on a journey to a whole new kingdom—one not of this earth.

Few journeys of importance are simple or easy, but as you gain altitude by climbing the mountain on this journey of honor, you'll understand that this is the greatest journey of your life.

There will be times when you question, times when you stand on the side of the mountain wondering, "Do I trust you, God?" Our lies and insecurities make that trust hard, but He is the only way to go to the next level. If we choose Him, with every slope we ascend, He unveils new beauty to us.

Let the words to this Planetshakers song, "Leave Me Astounded," encourage you:

> Leave me astounded, leave me amazed.
> Show off Your glory, let heaven invade.
> We're waiting with worship,
> We're waiting with praise
> For the Almighty presence of God to invade.

I remember when I arrived in New York City for the first time. People had told me how beautiful it was, but I arrived in the middle of a stormy, overcast day in summer. From ground level, riding in a cab, I couldn't see the lights or the towering buildings. People had talked about this city so much, but my first impression was that, from ground level, it wasn't as beautiful as they had said it would be.

The next morning, though the clouds were gone, I still couldn't see much from the streets between the enormous buildings. Then I visited the Empire State building. I took an elevator to the top to get beyond the street level view of cabs and trash and throngs of people—I needed to be elevated.

Everything looks different from the top of the Empire State building.

As I stepped onto the observation deck; I looked out and saw beauty everywhere. It took a journey to arrive there, but I saw the wonder of New York City from the Empire level.

Too many Christians view life only from the valley level. We let fears and lies and dishonor keep us at the lowest possible altitudes, when in actuality God is calling us to the heights. He is calling us to journey up the mountainside with Him, to trust Him to lead us along narrow trails that few ever experience.

Once you catch a view of life from the kingdom level, the beauty and wonder on the mountain, you'll never want to go back to the lower elevations. Promises and inheritance are on the horizon, visible as silver blessings when seen from the kingdom level. It's a beautiful horizon full of possibilities, but you'll never see it until you experience the journey of honor.

God urges you, "Come up here! Come up and see things from My perspective—from the kingdom level!"

You have a choice. Will you join God at the kingdom level?

Will you choose honor? Will you use the honor key to unlock a limitless life?

ACKNOWLEDGEMENTS

To my amazing wife, Sam—thank you for continually hungering for more of God and never settling down. This book is about our life together, which has been incredible so far. You truly are a powerful woman of God, and I love what God is doing through you.

To my children—thank you for being legendary kids. This book is partly about our journey together.

To my youth pastor, Danny Guglielmucci—thank you for believing in me and honoring the God in me.

To my brother, Ashley—thank you for being a great brother. You are doing amazing things for God.

To Dad—you're the best! Thank you for the heritage and inheritance you have provided for me.

To my mum in heaven—thank you for teaching me to love Jesus.

To our Planetshakers church—I am honored to lead the greatest people in the world!

To my executive members, board members, and all other teams who champion the vision day in and day out—thank you for trusting in my leadership.

To my publishers, influencers (Sol Arledge, Steve Blount, Susan Blount, Terri Gibbs, Eliza Delgado) and book team (John Mason and Josh Lease, Neil Smith, Joshua Brown, Estelle Lam, James Pilmer, and Leonie Smith)—thank you sincerely.

To my friends who have written books that have blessed me and to those who have so kindly written endorsements— thank you.

Finally and most importantly, thank you to my heavenly Father who loves and believes in me so much that He would use an insecure "pastor's kid" to touch so many people's lives. Thank you for honoring us by sending Jesus.

ABOUT THE AUTHOR

One of the leading international communicators of this generation, Russell Evans comes from a rich multigenerational ministry heritage. Prior to founding Planetshakers City Church in Melbourne, Australia, he served faithfully under his father's ministry at Paradise Church in Adelaide, South Australia. He has also served as the national leader of Australia's Youth Alive movement and has held a position as one of his denomination's state executives.

In February 2004, Russell, along with wife, Sam, founded the 10,000 member Planetshakers City Church. The annual conference, which has grown to over 25,000 attendees, donates millions of dollars each year to promote and sustain social justice around the world.

As founder and director of Planetshakers, Russell has an uncompromising desire to see every person make a difference in their world. Planetshakers is a global ministry phenomenon that has sold hundreds of thousands of praise and worship albums worldwide.

Enjoying close relationships with many of the world's leading ministers, Russell is well known for his collaborative approach to building God's kingdom. He has the rare capacity to relate equally to both younger and older generations of people due to his rich heritage and experience along with a passion for fresh music and empowerment of emerging leaders. He has committed his life to "empower generations to win generations."

Russell and his wife, Sam, live in Melbourne, Australia, with their two children, Jonathan and Aimee.

ABOUT PLANETSHAKERS

Under the leadership of Pastors Russell and Sam Evans, Planetshakers is a worldwide movement driven by a mandate to "empower generations to win generations." At its core, all ministry expressions seek first and foremost to pursue the presence of God and breakthrough anointing for people's lives. It is our deep desire that people discover their unique calling and God-given destiny.

All expressions of Planetshakers find their source in the local church in Melbourne, Australia, and Cape Town, South Africa. In ten short years God has blessed us with over 10,000 members. Our greatest priority and passion is to reach and impact our cities and see them transformed by the power of God and the love of God's people. To this end, Planetshakers is involved in numerous community and charitable causes including prison ministry, school programs, refugee outreach, disaster relief, and welfare assistance. Planetshakers also partners with World Vision to assist in urgent humanitarian crises around the world (www.planetshakersworldvision.com).

In addition to our annual event in Melbourne called *Awakening*, Planetshakers will hold sister events in Malaysia and the USA in 2014 with plans to extend to other nations (www.planetshakersawakening.com).

Planetshakers *band* tours the world continually, ministering to approximately one million people per year and bringing refreshment with its passionate breakthrough praise and worship experience. Each year Planetshakers band records a live CD and DVD. For booking inquiries please email touring@planetshakers.com.

Planetshakers *Kids Curriculum* has been carefully developed by our children's pastors to inspire and equip children's ministers to effectively reach the children God has entrusted to them. Written to accommodate the different learning styles of children, it includes artwork for RAM cards, color-ins, DVDs, posters, and much more.

It is our desire at *Planetshakers Kids* to provide Christ-centered, positive, and uplifting music, where kids of all ages not only have fun listening to the music, but also worship God and feel encouraged. We feel it is important to give kids music they are comfortable showing their unchurched friends, music that is just as relevant as what they might hear on any radio station, movie, or TV show. Jesus spoke the language of His day. He was culturally relevant, but He didn't water down the gospel message. We seek to do the same. It is our prayer that as your kids, grandkids, or friends listen to the music we have created, they will be drawn closer to God and biblical truths will be embedded deep in their lives, serving them well into adulthood. The CD is titled "Shout Praises Kids, Nothing Is Impossible" (in the USA and throughout the world) or "Planetshakers Kids Nothing Is Impossible" (in Australia and New Zealand). For more information please visit www.planetshakerskids.com.

Planetshakers *College* is based at our Melbourne campus and supports the vision by equipping local and international students to impact their world for Christ. For more information, please visit our website at www.planetshakers.com.

TO ORDER MORE COPIES

FOREWORD BY
JOHNBEVERE
BEST-SELLING **AUTHOR OF** *THE BAIT OF SATAN*

THE
HONOR
UNLOCK A
LIMITLESS
LIFE
KEY

RUSSELL
EVANS
planetshakers

To order more copies of this book,
visit www.myhealthychurch.com